GOING FROM
Glory
TO *Glory*

Going From Glory to Glory

Ava Fulmer

XULON PRESS

Xulon Press
2301 Lucien Way #415
Maitland, FL 32751
407.339.4217
www.xulonpress.com

© 2018 by Ava Fulmer

Edited by Xulon Press.

All rights reserved solely by the author. The author guarantees all contents are original and do not infringe upon the legal rights of any other person or work. No part of this book may be reproduced in any form without the permission of the author. The views expressed in this book are not necessarily those of the publisher.

Unless otherwise indicated, Scripture quotations taken from the Amplified Bible (AMP). Copyright © 1954, 1958, 1962, 1964, 1965, 1987 by The Lockman Foundation. Used by permission. All rights reserved.

Scripture quotations taken from the English Standard Version (ESV). Copyright © 2001 by Crossway, a publishing ministry of Good News Publishers. Used by permission. All rights reserved.

Scripture quotations taken from the King James Version (KJV) – *public domain.*

Scripture quotations taken from the Holy Bible, New International Version (NIV). Copyright © 1973, 1978, 1984, 2011 by Biblica, Inc.™. Used by permission. All rights reserved.

Printed in the United States of America.

ISBN-13: 978-1-54563-975-7

PREFACE

The winds were blowing so strong one could hardly stand up, snow was on the ground knee deep, and it was freezing. We had been released from school early that day due to a weather alert announcing a blizzard was fast approaching. Since we walked to and from school every day, my sister Kathy and I didn't think we needed to line up with those who rode the bus. In a panic, we grabbed hands and ran past the teachers out the door to hurry home.

Kathy decided we should not take our regular route and insisted she knew a shortcut. Little did we know, our parents had already been called to come to the school and pick us up. In no time, we were lost and not sure which direction to go as everything was one color: white. The wind was blowing so hard and the snow was falling so heavy that we could barely see. We fell into a deep pile of snow and could not get back up.

Crying and scared, we just knew we were going to die when, after what seemed like forever, a hand reached down and pulled us out. It was my father. It was a miracle he found us in the middle of a blizzard. That could have been the day of my demise, but God said, "Not so." He had another plan. Purpose kept us alive and destiny was calling. God appointed me to write this book and you to read it.

I invite you to come and walk with me through my journey of life from early childhood to adulthood, through sickness, loss, heartache, and pain. Guilt and condemnation almost destroyed me. I was convinced I could not go on, attempting to take my own life, but once again my Heavenly Father said, "Not so." Through it all, I came to know and experience God's unending love and His delivering power. I believe in sharing the real-life struggles one faces though walking with the Lord. It is my prayer this book will be a blessing to you and will encourage you to get up if you have fallen and to keep moving, always turning your eyes upon Jesus looking full into His wonderful face.

—Pastor Ava Fulmer

FOREWORD

This book is written as a means of encouragement for those who lack courage, as a tool of authenticity for those who lack the God kind of faith, and also as a guide for those who are weak in their spirit to promote strength and steadfastness.

Pastor Ava Fulmer tells the story of how she got from the starting point on her pathway of life to the current destination that God has mapped out for her in this season. It is our own story that helps others to follow God's road map. Will there be twist, turns and detours? Absolutely! Nevertheless, He assures us that we will make it to the very end. Pastor Ava's story tells us how God did it for her, one step at a time, from glory to glory.

—Phyllis Clemmons

ACKNOWLEDGMENTS

I want to first acknowledge my husband, Earl C. Fulmer, my chocolate honey. It is only because of his constant nudging that I was able to breathe life back into a manuscript that had been lying dormant on a shelf, collecting dust for many years. One day he handed it to me and said, "Do something with this manuscript, and do it now. Let's do whatever it takes to make this book happen." He was more excited than I was once we started the process. He's been so supportive and has continued to encourage me throughout this journey. I admire him for being a man of much faith. He is never moved by obstacles. He speaks the Word and keeps moving forward.

I must acknowledge my siblings Frank, Cynthia, and Michael Hornsby. They were also a great inspiration to me, each one giving me that fresh wind beneath my wings to soar to the finish line of this book project. They didn't even know that, when they set out to reach their goals, I said to myself, "If they can do it, so can I." In the middle of much adversity, as they walked through the pain of grief and loss, they all stepped out in faith and reached for their dreams.

Cynthia painstakingly took control of her health and lost a whopping 100 pounds. She set a goal to walk in her first 5K marathon, crossing the finish line thirty minutes sooner than she expected. She has since walked in three other marathons. Within the same time frame, she was able to reach another goal by becoming a licensed, certified life coach. Her motto is "Living Life and Loving It."

My brother Michael opened a martial arts school named, True Force Tae-Kwon-Do. He desires to instill in his students that positive thinking is a true force and to always do their best at whatever they put their hands to. In 2017, he was not only inducted into the Martial Arts Hall of Fame, but he received the high honor of being promoted to 7th Degree Grand Master. He has been in martial arts for thirty-five years and has won numerous state and national championships.

My brother Frank would give you the shirt off his back and take his last dime to make sure you had something to eat, even if he didn't. He launched a lifelong dream called Angel Works that helps people who are in need. He has written many songs and is working on getting them recorded. Though he faces many challenges, he never gives up on his dreams and aspirations.

Tonia Woolever is the first person the Lord assigned to help me with the book. The day I told her about my desire to write a book about what the Lord had done in my life, she got the typewriter out and started typing. That was when we still used typewriters. Tonia typed, proofread, and edited the first draft that was sent to the publishers many years ago. Thank you so much, Toni. I love and appreciate all you've done for me. You and Ron took me into your home at a very critical time in my life. You were the bridge to the next phase of my life.

The following are my sisters in Christ who are dear to my heart and are authors. You have indeed inspired me and are my heroes: Phyllis Clemmons (who is also my

Acknowledgments

editor/proofreader), Eagle Renata McWright, Rev. Cheryl Thompson, Apostle Mary Dixon, Rita Monroe and Apostle Melissa Weathersby (my writing coach). You all have set an example for me to follow.

I must acknowledge the mighty women of God, who have been an inspiration and many times the driving force that has caused me to soar to new heights in different seasons of my life. I've watched you continue to "press toward the mark of the high calling" as you continue to keep a praise on your lips. You all have exercised God's strength to stand, no matter what trials have come to knock you down. You have encouraged me, prayed for and with me, believed in me, and have been there for me. I thank the Lord for sending you into my life. Co-Pastor Portia Brooks Vaughn (also an author), I cannot thank the Lord enough for bringing you into my life. If it had not been for twenty-one years of your instruction, correction, teachings, love, and support, I would not be the woman of God that I am today. Chief-Apostle Rosa Wilson, Apostle Cindy Daniels, Elder Ethel Gathers, Dr. Dorinda Rolle, my aunt, Lillian Moore, Apostle Charlene Knight, and my dear friend Verna Harris, who has been my confidant and prayer partner for many years, I love you and will always be grateful to you and for you.

I want to acknowledge three of my dear friends. They are Teresa Robertson (my best friend when I was a teenager), Pat Stendebach and Grace Cunningham. They have always been there for me no matter what was going on in my world. Your friendship has meant the world to me. I want to acknowledge my church family, The Clarion Call Christian Center. I love you very much. Thank you for your prayers, love, and support. You were ever before me as I pressed to stay focused and finish this book. I hope

I am as much of a blessing to you as those mentioned above were to me. It is my prayer these testimonies will inspire you to keep moving, keep looking up, and to get up when you fall. Continue to always look to the hills from where your help comes. Keep striving to be and do all our Heavenly Father has ordained for your lives.

DEDICATION

I dedicate this book to my parents, Frank and Elena Hornsby. What can I say? There are really no words that can express why I must dedicate this book to them and acknowledge them. My father was my rock and my mother, my heart. I love them more than ever and still miss them terribly. Our home was full of love, discipline, and support. I believe I had the best parents ever. They have both left me with precious memories I will always cherish. I would not change anything about my upbringing. I am especially thankful for the values and the love for family they instilled in us. They are in heaven and have been gone for many years now. Our family still stands strong with a closer bond than ever.

I also dedicate this book to my sister Kathy Hornsby. I affectionately called her Kabers. While play-acting one day in our bedroom (something we did often during our childhood), Kathy said, "Ava you be Abers and I'll be Kabers" Thus those names became our nicknames for each other. She was not only my closest friend but also my cheerleader. The bond between us is indescribable. I can still hear her tell me I was her best friend. We remained close from early childhood until her death. She always believed in me and told me often I needed to write a book. I recently found a birthday card she gave me a few years ago. She signed it saying though she was the oldest, she looked up to me and I was her hero. I must say she was my hero.

Kathy accomplished everything she set her mind to do, becoming an actress and a playwright. She realized her calling to preach God's Word could be accomplished through the ministry of the theatrical stage and thus formed Player's in Christ and Hornsby Theatre and Entertainment. My admiration for Kathy grew even more when she went back to school in her fifties to obtain double master's degrees in education and theatre arts. I'm so thankful for the fun and loving memories I have of our time together. I never imagined we would not grow old together. Our Heavenly Father knew best and called her home at the age of sixty-two. Kathy, I will forever miss and love you, and I look forward to seeing you again.

Last but not least, I dedicate this book to my children. I love you with every beat of my heart. Thank you for the gift of grandchildren. They, too, are the loves of my life. One of my greatest desires has been to be a godly wife and mother and that you will carry out the legacy of my faith. I pray this book will encourage you to continue walking in all I have poured into you and that you will trust in the Lord with all of your heart, keeping Him in the center of your life all of your days.

CONTENTS

1. Angel Child 1
2. From Darkness to Light. 8
3. Condemned 16
4. Old Things Pass Away; All Things Become New 20
5. Joy Comes in the Morning 28
6. The Pink Angel 37
7. His Healing and Power of Protection 44
8. A State of Depression 51
9. A Broken Dream 60
10. A Change of Pace 69
11. His Miracles Never Cease 76
12. He Will Perfect That Which Concerns You . . 79
13. He Supplies All My Needs 82
14 We Are More Than Conquerors. 91

Chapter 1

Angel Child

"Your daughter has spinal meningitis, Mr. and Mrs. Hornsby. She probably won't live through the night." After doing everything they could to break my fever, my parents decided to take me back to the hospital one more time.

My father was stationed at Andrew Air Force Base in Washington, DC, but we lived off base miles away from the base hospital. It was very cold outside and snowing. My fever was so high the doctor decided the best treatment for me was to be placed in a tub of ice water every hour on the hour. The fever steadily continued to climb and would not break. The doctor told my parents there was nothing else they could do and for them to take me home and wait for me to die. According to my mother, the doctors said I would let out a loud scream just before expiring.

After driving home on that cold snowy night, my parents prayed and fearfully placed me in my crib. Hours later, just as the doctor had predicted, I let out a loud scream. Panic stricken, they ran to my crib expecting to find me dead. Instead, I had stopped screaming, and I was looking up at them smiling. At that moment, mother said, "Oh, my little Angel Child!" This became my nickname. I was three months old then, and that was to be the first of many miracles the Lord would perform in my life.

I was born on June 7, 1956, in Washington, DC, the second oldest child out of eight children. My father, Frank E. Hornsby, Jr. was serving in the United States Air Force at that time. I always loved to see my father in his uniform. We were transferred to a different base just about every two years. We'd also previously lived in Nashville, Tennessee; Chicago, Illinois; Rapid City, South Dakota; Biloxi, Mississippi; Shreveport, Louisiana; and Anchorage, Alaska.

My favorite place was Alaska. It was beautiful! We were surrounded by spectacular snow-capped mountains all year long. Believe it or not, I loved the cold! We played outside almost every day, regardless of the temperature. My favorite activity was ice skating.

I loved traveling around from state to state. There was only one drawback. Just as I began developing close relationships with classmates and had made a new best friend, it would be time to move again. I can remember sadly waving goodbye to friends and wondering if I would ever see them again. My parents, on the other hand, made long-lasting friendships with people they met on each base and stayed in touch with them for years. There were a couple of families who also moved to San Antonio after retiring. We found out that we had all settled in the same state, same city, and the same neighborhood.

My father was a strict disciplinarian. However, he loved us dearly and always took us on fun outings. He was a great cook, and sometimes he would spend the day cooking us a special meal "just because." My mother was very warm and caring. She also loved us deeply and poured her life into caring for all of us. Both of my parents would pour their efforts into making each holiday one we would never forget.

My mother would not tolerate sibling rivalry under any circumstance. If we bickered with each other, she would put us in the bathroom together, and we could not come out until we were ready to make up and show our heartfelt affection with genuine hugs and kisses.

We were raised in a home with Christian values. My mother saw to it that we were in church every Sunday. The only excuse for missing church was illness or a family emergency. If my mother did not go to church, we would have church at home. She would gather all of her children together in a circle. We would sing a song or two, and then my mother would read a scripture and say a prayer. We also took communion. She would make grape Kool-Aid and break up some crackers for the communion. This is one of the many precious childhood memories I will always treasure.

Another cherished memory I have is that whenever I would get sick, my mother would always cuddle me in her arms. She would pray for me and then sing a song entitled, "God Will Take Care of You." I can still hear the beginning of the song in my mind to this day. "Be not dismayed, whatever may be, God will take care of you." I also remember my mother taking me for walks. She would sing another song I grew to love: "In the Garden." She sang, "He walks with me and He talks with me and He tells me I am His own." It was my favorite line in the song.

As a small child, I can remember having a sense of God and His presence. When I was about eight years old, I vividly remember having my first encounter with the Lord. We were living in Alaska at that time. I was at school and was not feeling well. My teacher sent me to the school nurse and although I was spiking a fever, my father was not able to leave work to come and pick me up. School was going to be out soon anyway, so the nurse took me to a small, quiet room and had me lay down.

I specifically remember her turning off the light and closing the door. The room was dark. I fell asleep. While I slept, I sensed someone hovering over me. It seemed as if they were sitting on the bed next to me. I woke up. I know I was fully awake and not asleep. As I opened my eyes, the light in the room was very bright. I knew it was not the same light that was in the room when I first entered it but a different kind of light.

It was much brighter, and there was something special about it. I knew no one had opened the door, so the light was not coming from the hallway. I looked down at the end of my bed, and there was an altar set up with a Bible in the center of it. For some reason, I began to cry. I wasn't crying because I was sad or afraid but because of the Spirit that was in the room. There was so much love and peace. There was a figure standing in the light that was also part of the light.

I don't know how I knew; I just seemed to know that it was Jesus. He was revealing His love for me. Suddenly, the door swung open and the room became dark again. I knew then that the light in the room had been from another source other than the light switch. The nurse turned the light on and told me school was out.

I didn't tell anyone about my divine encounter with the Lord because I was not really sure what just happened. I just knew something supernatural had taken place. The experience stayed with me for the rest of the day and well into the night. I didn't know it then, but as I look back over my life now, there were many times when I would need to be reminded of the great love I felt that day. That love would be the very thing the devil would do his best to make me forget.

I always believed in God, but I would have believed in Muhammed had my parents taught me to. I thought everyone believed in God or that all people in America were Christians. To me, it was just like believing in the flag. I thought everyone went to school Monday through Friday and went to church on Sunday.

In 1969, my father decided to retire from the Air Force, and we moved from Louisiana to San Antonio, Texas. My dad had to stay in Louisiana for six months while we went to Texas ahead of him. My father kept the car with him, which left us without transportation. If we wanted to go anywhere, we walked or called our relatives. We lived on the northwest side of the city, near a church that was within walking distance of our house. The high school was also within walking distance.

My mother wanted us in church, but the all-black churches were on the other side of town. We were used to going to church at the chapel on base for the twenty-one years my father was in the military. There were only two choices: go to the Catholic service or the Protestant service where the services were always multi-racial. The only reason my mother was concerned about attending an all-black church is we had just left a very prejudiced Louisiana. The blacks stayed on one side of the street, and the whites stayed on the other side. I can remember my father being very upset when he found out the school we had to attend was not on the military base.

This was the first time we would have to attend school off base. I remember the time when one of my friends, who attended the school but lived off base, asked her mother if

I could come home with her on Friday and spend the night. Although her mother told her "no" several times, eventually she relented and allowed me to come for an overnight stay. We had been playing outside for about an hour when her mother came to the door and insisted that we come inside. Her mother was visibly upset. We wondered if we had done something wrong.

The phone was ringing when we came inside. Carlene's mother answered the phone and after a short conversation, she hung up the phone. She was in tears. She appeared angry and disturbed. She quickly hustled us upstairs to the bedroom with no explanation. Only minutes after going upstairs, we heard a loud scream. Someone had driven by their home holding a sign. It read, "Get that nigger out of our neighborhood!"

They proceeded to throw an object into the front yard that burst into flames when it hit the ground. I can't remember the details of how the fire was extinguished. I do remember that the fire never reached the house. The next thing I knew, my father was at the door. He had come to pick me up. My friend was crying and could not understand why I had to go home. Her mother was still quite distressed. She tearfully kept apologizing to my father as she put me in the car.

My friend told me on the following Monday at school that her mother told her we could not be friends anymore. Carlene said she did not care what happened, I would always be her friend. We still played together during recess and sat together for lunch.

Since my mother was not sure of the racial situation in San Antonio, she wrote a letter to the pastor of the church that was within walking distance from our house, Marbach Christian Church. The pastor's name was T. E. Veale. She explained in the letter that we were a black family that was new to the area and that she wanted her children to attend church. She stated in the letter that although we were without transportation, she thought it was close enough for us to walk the distance to the church. My mother asked if we had permission to attend at least until we got transportation and could go on the other side of town where the black churches were.

As told to me by members of Marbach at that time, the pastor read the letter to the congregation. After reading the letter, he told (not asked) the congregation to welcome our family with open arms. One day, soon after my mother had mailed the letter, there was a knock on our door. A family that attended the church was standing on the other side of the door with a meal, a cake, and some other goodies. They introduced themselves and told us they had come to let us know not only were we welcome to attend the church, but there would be someone at our house on Sunday mornings to give us a ride.

When we met Brother Veale, the pastor, face-to-face, he hugged us all like we were family. He, along with the other members of that church, showed us so much love. It was the love of Jesus I saw in them—the same love of Jesus that I saw in my mother that aided me in coming to the Lord and accepting Him as my Savior.

Chapter 2

From Darkness to Light

Up until the age of twelve, I was basically a good child and didn't get into much trouble. I respected my parents and obeyed them most of the time. However, as I entered the 7th grade, I began to think they were just too strict, especially my father. When I turned thirteen, I became rebellious. I remember talking back to my mother one day, and my dad reacted so fast! He let us know this kind of behavior would not be tolerated. When we were disciplined, we either felt the wrath of the belt, or we were severely punished (restricted) for an extended period of time. My mother was very soft spoken. She loved being a mother. If she had to get after us with a belt, she would start crying.

As we got older, she would scold us and then finish her sentence by saying, "I'm just going to wait until your father gets home and tell him about it." We would beg her not to tell Dad; we would take whatever punishment she thought was appropriate. We would even go get the belt for her and beg her, "Please don't tell Dad!" When Dad had to whip us, I can remember him saying with each lick, "This hurts me more than it does you. If I didn't love you I wouldn't whip you." I always wondered, *If it hurt him more than it hurt me, why was I the one crying*? I had wonderful parents, and I was thankful to God for them. I loved them very much but did not really appreciate their discipline until after I became a parent myself.

I was so rebellious for a period of time that my parents threatened to put me in a private school for girls. Well, that got my attention! *No boys*? Oh no, that just could not happen! Boys seemed to be all I thought about. They had my attention, and I knew I had theirs. My dad used to introduce me to his friends and say, "This is Ava. She is thirteen, going on twenty, and is majoring in boys."

One day after school as I waited to catch the bus home from Sul Ross Middle School, I met a boy named Thomas Earl Burton. Two of his brothers attended school there, and he had come to pick them up. Thomas was extremely good-looking. . He walked up to me and asked where he could find his brothers. I thought I was going to pass out. We hooked up that day. I was thrilled when he asked me for my phone number. He was seventeen years old and a senior in high school. Of course, I did not give the age difference any thought, nor did I give any thought to what my parents would think. I fell head over heels in love with him. I thought the sun, the moon, and the earth revolved around him. He was not only good-looking but very charming as well.

When Thomas met my mother, he was so charming, she too forgot how old he was, and she agreed to let me talk to him on the phone. If he was going to be at any parties I was invited to, she volunteered to help chaperone them. However, when my dad found out about him and how old he was, he hit the roof and forbade me to have any contact with him. I didn't allow that to stop me, though. Thomas continued to come to the school to see me. Sometimes, he would offer to give me a ride home, and we would stay behind the bus so that when I got out of his car, it would appear as though I had gotten off the bus.

In the meantime, some of my friends at school had started experimenting with drugs. I remember the popular thing was to mix pills in your soda, preferably Coca Cola, so the teachers would have no idea the Coke you were drinking for lunch had drugs in it. Also, it seemed like every time I went to the doctor, no matter the diagnosis, I was given a prescription of Darvon, Valium, and codeine cough syrup. I only took the pills if I had gotten in trouble at home and was mad at my parents.

One day I took something someone gave me. I didn't know what it was, but they convinced me I would love how it made me feel. I was so high in school, I could hardly walk down the hall. If someone asked me what was wrong, I would say, I wasn't feeling good. I really hated how it made me feel and hoped it would hurry up and wear off. One of my class mates told Thomas I was taking drugs and how I was walking around like I was drunk. He called me up, upset about it, and told me he did not want to have anything to do with someone on drugs.

I tried to explain to him that I didn't really like how the pills made me feel, and I would not be taking them anymore. He broke up with me anyway. He not only broke up with me, but he called my parents and told them I was taking drugs and getting them from someone at my school. My dad went to the school the next day and told the principal about the phone call he had gotten from my boyfriend. I was called to the office and had to tell them who had given me the pills or I would be suspended for taking drugs on campus.

I just knew my father was going to let me have it on the way home from school that day and that restriction or a whipping would follow when I got home. But my parents didn't say a word. I think they felt it was punishment enough knowing my boyfriend had called them. I was embarrassed and heartbroken. I was confused and disillusioned about drugs. Eventually, I just lost interest in them.

Thomas had really done me a favor. It was all part of God's divine intervention in my life. It didn't feel good at the time, and I would not understand until later in life why things worked out as they had, but it was the best thing for me. Romans 8:28 says, "And we know that in all things, God works for the good of those who love Him, who have been called according to His purpose" (NIV). The breakup with Thomas and his call to my parents definitely worked for my good.

I decided I was going to make some life-changing decisions in my 8th-grade year. I became very active in the youth group at Marbach Christian Church. My family had been so well accepted there that we joined the church and stayed active members for many years.

Every summer in Center Point, Texas, all the Disciples of Christ churches in other cities throughout Texas, gathered together for a week-long Christian Family Camp. I had heard many stories from the youth group about how much fun it was and how it would be the experience of a lifetime. I wanted to go, but we just could not afford it. One day, my pastor called and said if I wanted to go, someone had offered me a scholarship. I was thrilled.

Since I had never been to camp before, I really had no idea what to expect. What I found when I got to camp was life changing. I had been in church all my life. I considered myself to be a Christian. My mother was always teaching us about God and His love. But I was about to learn that I knew of Jesus but did not know Him as my personal Savior and Lord.

The camp started on a Sunday and ended the following Saturday. There was a 7 a.m. gathering for prayer and meditation. Only a few of the children and teenagers attended this early morning meditation service, but I didn't want to miss anything, so I got up early so I could be there. Afterward, we had breakfast, followed by a gathering of all camp participants for morning praise and worship. Later, we were divided up according to our age categories.

Everyone had activities according to their age group, adults as well as the children and teens. After lunch, everyone was expected to participate in "horizontal hour," which was a fancy terminology that meant it was nap time. The remainder of the afternoon was filled with recreational activities such as swimming, games, and shopping trips to town.

The evening time was my favorite. We would meet again under the open tabernacle after dinner for more praise and worship and teaching of the Word of God. Each night, there was a different preacher speaking. In these evening services, it seemed that something supernatural always took place. The atmosphere was charged with excitement, and the presence and power of God fell like I had not witnessed before.

These services started around 7 p.m. and would end around 9:30 p.m. Afterward, the Lord continued to move. People stayed at the altar praying. They would often break out into small groups throughout the camp, sharing what the Lord had done for them during the service. Some of the groups would just sing the songs of Zion. Sometimes the anointing of the Lord would linger until well past midnight.

From Darkness To Light

The people at camp were so full of joy. They had such an excitement about them. When they were singing, they would clap their hands, raise their arms, and shout for joy. I had not experienced anything like that before. One thing I knew was that they were genuine and sincere in their love for God. Everyone hugged each other and spoke of their love for one another. They prayed about everything! When they prayed, it was with great faith, and when a prayer was finished, everyone acted like they knew the prayer was already answered.

I was in awe of it all. It made me realize I was missing something very profound and significant in my life, and I wanted what they had. I didn't know what it was, but whatever it was, I wanted it! I began to understand that these people had a relationship with Jesus. I believed in Him, but I didn't have a relationship with Him.

On Wednesday night, at the end of the message, the speaker gave an invitation to come to the altar. It wasn't an invitation to join a church as I had witnessed in the past. Instead it was to ask Jesus to come into their hearts and take complete control of their lives. The preacher invited those of us who knew Jesus as Savior to ask Him to become Lord of our lives as well. I knew right away I wanted that, and I ran to the altar. I couldn't seem to stop crying as I asked Jesus to come into my heart, take me as I was, and be my Lord.

The song "Just as I Am" was being sung over and over. I was instructed to pray and ask for forgiveness of my sins. As I prayed, suddenly I felt the Lord engulf me with His love. It was as if He was holding me in His arms. It felt as if there was a carafe of warm oil being poured all over me. Tears streamed down my face, not because I was afraid or hurt, but because of the love I felt deep inside. It was the same love I felt in the room when I was a little girl and I was at school in the little room where the nurse took me to lay down until school was out.

I knew the Lord had touched me. I can't even describe the joy I felt. None of the pills I took ever gave me this level of euphoria of joy and peace. When I finally got up from that altar, I knew I was forever changed. I had passed from darkness into Light.

> Again Jesus spoke to them, saying, I am the light of the world. Whoever follows me will not walk in darkness, but will have the light of life (John 8:12 ESV).

> You are a chosen generation, a royal priesthood, a holy nation, His own special people, that you may proclaim the praises of Him who called you out of darkness into His Marvelous light. (1 Peter 2:9 KJV)

When I returned home from camp, I was on fire for the Lord! I wanted to tell everyone and anyone who would listen about Jesus and how He had changed my life. I felt like I was in love. Thoughts about Jesus and the love I felt for Him and He for me was always on my mind. My parents, especially my brothers and sisters, thought I had gone bonkers. I could not put the Bible down. I was like a sponge soaking up water. Sometimes I would open the Bible and read something at random, and it would be as if Jesus was talking directly to me. The verse I was reading always fit whatever I was going through or was praying about.

About two weeks after returning from camp, my sister Kathy and I were invited to a party given by some high school friends. As soon as I walked through the door, I knew the change in me was real. I felt like a fish out of water. I no longer belonged. Someone handed me a drink. I wondered where the parents were because everyone was drinking alcohol. I took one sip and looked at the glass and said to myself, "I don't want this, and I don't want to be here." The party was just down the street from where we lived. I told my sister I would see her later and went home.

Going to church was even different. The songs, the prayers, and the sermons came alive, and I began to understand them better. Although I had been in church all my life, for the first time, it all had real meaning. I looked forward to every Sunday. It was as if I had been given new eyes and ears to hear and understand His Word. Everything about me had changed. It was as if I had been looking at everything through dark glasses, and now suddenly, I was able to see things more clearly.

> Now the Lord is that Spirit and where the Spirit of the Lord is, there is liberty. But we all, with open face beholding as in a glass the glory of the Lord, are changed into the same image from glory to glory, even as by the Spirit of the Lord. (2 Corinthians 3:17–18 KJV)

Chapter 3

Condemned

At the beginning of my freshman year in high school, I became president of the youth group. Our youth group was on fire for the Lord. We were very close and had so much fun together. We participated in a lot of activities. I loved our Tuesday night youth prayer meeting. It was so exciting to hear how prayers prayed the week before had been answered. We would sing and worship the Lord, share testimonies, and pray for our individual needs.

Though I thought I would never get over Thomas Earl, the boy who broke my heart in 7th grade, I found I was still "boy crazy" as my dad would always describe me. I loved the Lord with all my heart, but by this time the boys were running a close race for first place in my heart. One day one of my classmates introduced me to a young man named Verlon. Was he in the 9th grade? Of course, he wasn't. Here I go again. He was nineteen years old and in the military.

Verlon had just finished basic training. He also had earned his black belt in karate. I was so impressed. Verlon was "drop-dead" gorgeous, suave, and charming. Good looking and charming was a combination I just could not resist.

I think I figured if the boys who were older chose me over some of the girls their own age, then they must really like me. I just knew I must have had something the other girls didn't have. Being convinced of this way of thinking was the first lie the enemy used as part of his destructive plan for me. According to my sisters, I was very vain and stayed in the mirror, constantly combing my hair, checking my makeup, and making sure the outfit I was wearing was just right. I remember I would not even go to the mailbox to check the mail, unless my hair was freshly combed, I had my makeup on, and I had put on the right outfit. If we were making plans to go somewhere, and there were going to be boys, I definitely wanted to go.

Verlon was like a "play son" to a couple who were friends of my parents, so they allowed him to come over and visit with me. He was also friends with my brother, Frank. My parents would let me go with Verlon if it was with a group of other kids. I don't think they realized we were "going together" and that I was completely smitten. One night he talked me into getting away from the crowd alone. I remember that he told he wanted to spend time with me alone.

We left the others at the movies, and he took me back to the base where he was stationed. He told me he wanted to show me the barracks where he stayed. I was a little nervous about it because I wasn't supposed to be out with him alone and away from the group I left the house with. My parents thought I was at the movies; instead I was somewhere else, and I was afraid of getting into trouble. He promised me we would not be gone long. He turned on the charm, telling me how much he loved me.

No one was in the barracks, and for some reason all the lights were out. He led me to a bed and convinced me to lay down with him for just a little while so we could talk. I really began to get nervous and kept saying he needed to take me home. But with his smooth talking and charming personality, he knew just what to say to calm me down. He began to kiss me all over and asked me if I loved him. Hesitantly, I said, "Yes." He convinced me to show him how much, and he enticed me into having sex with him. As soon as it was over, I felt something happen inside of me. I pushed him away and started crying. Everything happened so fast. I felt separated from God right away. I knew what I had done was wrong and that I had violated something very precious. I insisted he hurry up and take me back. Once we were in the car, no words passed between us.

The next day, I cried off and on all day. I kept telling myself, *Oh, no I've committed the unforgiveable sin.* At least I thought it was unforgiveable and that I had ruined the most important thing to me, my relationship with the Lord. I felt unclean and dirty. Asking Jesus to forgive me would have been sufficient, but I kept hearing a voice in my head tell me I was dirty now, and because of my sin, God did not love me anymore.

I wanted to pray and run back into the loving arms of Jesus. I was so depressed. This feeling of condemnation went on for several months. I started taking downers and codeine cough syrup just to be able to sleep at night. My outgoing personality, along with my ability to conceal my true feelings, helped me to dupe everyone into thinking all was well with me. No one knew how miserable I really was.

The guilt and condemnation was almost unbearable. I wanted so badly to talk to someone about what I was going through, but I was too ashamed. I should have gone to my pastor or our youth leader. Either one of those leaders would have given me the listening ear I so desperately needed. Perhaps, if I had been brave enough to tell someone what I was going through, they would have reminded me of God's unending love and forgiveness, as well as His promise to never leave me nor forsake me.

They could have also shared with me the scripture in the book of Romans 8:1 (NKJV):

> There is therefore now no condemnation to them which are in Christ Jesus, who walk not according to the flesh but according to the Spirit.

That same chapter explains that there is nothing that can separate me from Christ. I had experienced this love when I gave my life to Christ, but Satan laid a good trap for me and then lied to me, telling me God did not love me anymore. In John 10:10 (NKJV) it says, "The thief does not come except to steal, and to kill and to destroy. I have come that they may have life and that they may have it more abundantly."

To make matters worse, Verlon wasn't coming around that much anymore. I had only seen him maybe once or twice since the day he took me to the barracks. A couple of weeks later, while at school, I looked up and saw him walking down the hall toward me. I got so excited because I just knew he was there to see me. As he walked by, he barely spoke to me. His eyes were focused on another girl standing further down the hallway. They walked off together, holding hands. I was crushed. I remembered that, just a couple of weeks before, he told me he loved me. I stood there feeling stupid, embarrassed, and condemned.

Chapter 4

Old Things Pass Away; All Things Become New

*I*t was time for Christian Family Camp again. I was still convinced my relationship with the Lord was ruined. I was torn about going. It was the last day of camp registration before I decided I would go. My rationale was that I'd go just to see all of my friends. We had kept in touch with each other throughout the year, and as a result, a close bond had developed between us.

In the meantime, prior to going back to camp, I had been very sick. I was very weak and had not been able to hold down any food or water. One day, after I fainted, my mother took me to the doctor. One of the first questions the doctor asked after hearing my symptoms was, "Could you be pregnant?" I was shocked. Why was he asking me that question? I emphatically said, "Of course not!" I didn't want to consider that possibility and besides, surely if I was pregnant, I would not be as sick as I had been.

My mother never seemed to be that sick when she was pregnant. My mother was just as shocked as I was by the doctor's question and told the doctor she was sure pregnancy was not the problem. The doctor decided to run some tests. He also gave me some medicine for the nausea. He told us the test results would not be back for at least a week, so I would not know the results until I got back from camp.

On the first day of camp, I was glad to see everyone. Although I was feeling terribly nervous, I was so happy I had decided to come after all. I could not understand why I was feeling this way. I was curious to see if everyone still had that same joy and exuberance for the Lord they had the year before, and they did! They were still on fire for the Lord and full of so much love and joy. I was able to hide how miserable I was on the inside and that I felt very far away from God.

The first couple of days of camp, I was able to sit through all the meetings without falling apart or giving away my true feelings. I would psych myself up and try to turn off all my emotions. I wanted so desperately to return to the Lord, but since I thought I couldn't, I tried to harden my heart against Him. I still was not feeling good and kept getting sick to my stomach. By midweek, there was a war going on inside of me. I was a basket case. By then I had been on the verge of tears all day. That evening, when it was time for the evening tabernacle meeting, I decided to sit on the last row in the back by myself.

I was not sure if I was going to sit through the entire service. About halfway through the service, I heard an audible voice on my left side saying, "Ava, why don't you get up and leave! Jesus does not love you anymore. Remember what you did? You cannot be forgiven for it." Then in my right ear, I heard an audible voice also, but this voice was soft, gentle, and calm, saying to me, "Ava,

I love you. Come to me." I got up, walked out, and ran to my dorm.

By the time I got there, I had decided I wanted to go home, and I was going to call my father and ask him to come and pick me up. But something kept drawing me back, and I found myself walking back to the tabernacle. When I got there, I sat down on the same bench. It happened again. I heard a very desperate and condemning voice insisting that I leave saying, "You can't ever go back to Jesus." Afterward, on the other side I would hear the calm, gentle, and loving voice saying, "I love you, Ava. Come to me." This happened at least four times. I started sobbing so hard I just wanted to scream.

I stood up again with the intentions of leaving once and for all. Instead, I ran to my pastor, Bro. Veale. Let me take a moment to talk about this man, T. E Veale. He was the most loving man I had ever met. He always exemplified the character of Christ. He loved our family, and even after I went away to college and my family eventually left Marbach Christian Church, he remained very close to our family and was there for every crisis. He married me and was there when both of my parents died. He has since gone on to glory when he was in his nineties. I loved him very much.

The sermon was over, and they started singing the song, "Just as I Am." As I heard the words to the song, my heart begin to soften and my soul was saying yes to the words I was hearing:

> Just as I am without one plea
> But that thy blood was shed for me
> And that thou bid me come to Thee,
> O Lamb of God, I come! I come!

Old Things Pass Away; All Things Become New

 Just as I am and waiting not

To rid my soul of one dark blot;
To thee whose blood can cleanse each spot,
O Lamb of God, I come I come.

This verse set me free:

Just as I am, though tossed about
With many a conflict, many a doubt.
Fighting within and fears without,
O Lamb of God, I come, I come.

 When I ran over to Bro. Veale, I almost collapsed. I was going through what I know now to be deliverance. There was a tug of war going on for my life that night in spiritual warfare. Bro. Veale carried me to the altar. I was suddenly surrounded by people who began to pray for me. My best friend, Teresa Robertson, was next to me. She was always there when I needed her.
 They began praying for me in different languages. Suddenly, something rose up inside of me that wanted to fight them and tell them to shut up. I heard myself say, "*No! Leave me alone!*" It was like I didn't want to hear them pray. During all of this, I got sick to my stomach, but the men kept praying for me as if nothing had happened. Someone handed me something to wipe my mouth. Then, someone, with such boldness and authority, started rebuking and binding the devil. I had never heard anyone pray like that before. He said he discerned a spirit of condemnation and took authority over it, commanding it to let go of me and leave in the name of Jesus. I went limp and passed out again, only this time it was different.

I felt all the turmoil that had been inside of me leave. I knew all the heavy weight I had been carrying was gone. I was "slain in the spirit," an experience whereby God's power is so strong and prevalent, it is more than your physical body can bear. It was not painful or unpleasant. The "war" was over. I was literally drained from the battle. When the spirit of condemnation was called out and commanded to let me go, I heard a loud sound as if horses were running away. I felt much lighter, and I knew the burden of my sin was finally lifted.

My pastor asked me if I wanted to receive the baptism of the Holy Spirit. I didn't know what that was, but if it was what they had, I wanted it! He gently explained when I asked Jesus to come into my heart as my Savior, the Holy Spirit came in and was dwelling inside of me and had been there all along. To be baptized in the Holy Spirit meant I would receive power from God. He read from the Bible about how the disciples were asked to go to the upper room and wait for the promise and how, when it came like a mighty rushing wind, they received power and spoke in other tongues.

This prayer language was a gift from the Holy Spirit. I wanted all that the Lord wanted me to have, especially if this was a gift to me from Him. I will never forget what I experienced. Like before, it was as if warm oil was being poured all over me, that same warm oil I felt when I asked Jesus to come into my heart. I began to speak in tongues, and I could not stop laughing. The joy was overflowing and bubbling up inside of me. I felt drunk but not the drunk you feel from drinking alcohol.

Just as the men stopped praying for me, a man with red tennis shoes came up to me and put his hand on my head. He said, "My child, I give you peace." Everything in me was stilled. The peace I felt was indescribable. I had peace in body, my mind (no more evil voices), and peace in my spirit. It was all over me. It was the third day of camp. I had never seen this man before.

When everything was over and it was time to go to our dorms and time for "lights out," I wanted to thank the man who had on the red tennis shoes and tell him about the peace I felt when he laid his hands on my head. My friend, Teresa who had been sitting with me the whole time I was being prayed for, insisted there was no man that came up to me with red tennis shoes. I told everyone I could about him because who could miss a man wearing red tennis shoes? He walked up through all of the people surrounding me and put his hands on my head. No one remembers seeing that happen, but no one could convince me I had not seen it.

Looking back, I believe it was an angel. The Bible tells us in Hebrews 13:2 (KJV), "Be not forgetful to entertain strangers, for thereby some have entertained angels unawares."

Later that night, after lights out and just as I was drifting off to sleep, I heard music. It sounded like an orchestra of hallelujahs. It was the most beautiful music I had ever heard. I know I clearly heard it, but no one else did. I got up and went outside to look around, so I could find who was singing, but the campgrounds were dark and quiet. Everyone had gone to bed. When I went back inside, I decided to lay back down. One of the ladies came over to me and asked me if I still heard the music. When I told her yes, she said that the music was just for me, and the Lord was doing something supernatural by allowing me alone to hear it.

It was a "host of His angels, sent to minister to me," she said. The lady told me to just lie down and enjoy it. I finally drifted off to sleep, listening to the beautiful music.

The following morning, one of the men who had prayed for me the night before came up to me and told me he had a word from the Lord for me. The Lord told him to tell me that He had made me into a brand-new person, as if I were just born. Praise God! That was just what I needed to hear. I knew the man had heard from the Lord because he had no idea of the torment I had been experiencing over the past few months. I had not told anyone about it. To hear this word from the Lord, let me know that Jesus no longer remembered the sin I thought I could not be forgiven for. Once, I prayed for His forgiveness, He washed me clean again and made me brand new. If I was a new person, then that meant it was as if the sin I had committed had never happened. This was good news to me. Not only had the Lord delivered me from a spirit of guilt and condemnation, He had set me free and filled me with His precious Holy Spirit. In addition, He gave me my prayer language.

I was in Christ, I was a new person. In 2 Corinthians 5:17(KJV), it states "For old things are passed away; behold all things are become new." I love to share this scripture with others because I experienced being made brand-new first hand.

Another one of my favorite scriptures says, "His steadfast love is new every morning" (Lamentations 3:22–23). Only Jesus can make you brand-new again! No longer could Satan condemn me or make me feel guilty.

While reading my Bible that same day, I found the scripture that says, "There is therefore now no condemnation to those who are in Christ Jesus" (Romans 3:22–23

KJV). Satan could no longer lie to me and tell me I could not be forgiven. Psalm 103:10–12 states:

> He hath not dealt with us after our sins; nor rewarded us according to our iniquities. For as the heaven is high above the earth, so great is his mercy toward them that fear him. As far as the east is from the west, so far hath he removed our transgressions from us.

My sins were forgiven and forgotten!

Let me encourage you! Don't ever let the devil beat you up because of sins you have committed! The Bible tells us *all* have sinned and fallen short. Confess your sin and ask His forgiveness. The Bible teaches us to confess the sin and then repent. That means to turn around and go in another direction. Remember, the blood He shed on the cross was so that you could be forgiven for that sin. It's not just important to confess the sin and to ask for forgiveness, but it is just as important *to receive* that forgiveness.

The Lord loves you, and He promises to never leave you or forsake you. He also promises you that once you are His child, there is nothing, absolutely nothing, that can snatch you out of His hand and separate you from His love.

Chapter 5

Joy Comes In the Morning

I came back from camp excited and rejuvenated. I was determined not to forget how the Lord revealed to me that I was brand-new, and I felt as if I were brand-new. Little did I know, that word was going to have to carry me through what I was about to find out when I got home. I was still having trouble keeping food down and feeling weak from time to time. It had been a little over a week, so the doctor was due to call any day with the results from the tests he ran before I left for camp. The question he asked me, "Could you be pregnant?" continued to come to the forefront of my mind. I really had not suspected it, except once, but the thought was too dreadful to consider, so I pushed it out of my mind.

It was a Monday evening about 5:30 p.m. My dad had just gotten home from work when the phone rang. He reached over to pick it up from its cradle. I could tell by the look on his face and the tone of his voice something was terribly wrong. My heart skipped a couple of beats. When my father hung up the phone, he gave me the worst look as he picked up his keys from the kitchen table, walked out of the house, and drove off without a word. I had an awful feeling in the pit of my stomach. Suddenly, I was afraid. I knew what the doctor said.

Everything around me seemed suspended in space. I wanted to cry, but I couldn't. My father was gone for about thirty minutes. It seemed like hours to me. Just before he pulled into the drive way, I heard the voice of Jesus say to me once again, "You are a new person in Christ." I was not going to let this situation crumble me. The guilt and condemnation was gone. I was reminded of the scripture in Romans 8:1(KJV): "There is now no condemnation to those who are in Christ Jesus."

When my father finally came home, he was furious. He demanded that I come in the living room and sit down. I can still hear the words, "Ava, the doctor said you are pregnant." I froze. I did not want to believe it. He said he left the house earlier to go calm down to keep from killing me. He started fussing, but I was so stunned that I don't remember anything he said.

Afterward, he left the house again. When he returned my mother was with him. I was still sitting in the same spot I was in when he left. I just sat there not knowing what to do. When my mother came in, she just looked at me with tears in her eyes. She never said one condemning word to me. She didn't say anything. I was hurting but not for myself. I was hurting for the pain and anguish I caused my parents. I hated that I had disappointed them.

Seeing the tears in my mother's eyes was hard for me to bear. Everyone was quiet the rest of the evening. There was no conversation at the dinner table that night. I praise God for my parents. In spite of everything, my mother remained very loving and gentle. My father, on the other hand, had no tolerance for disrespect or disobedience.

When using the belt to discipline us, he never failed to remind us it was because he loved us.

The next few days, I walked around in a fog. I was just numb. My parents had not talked to me much at all. My siblings didn't say much to me, either. I am not sure if they knew what was going on. My oldest sister, Kathy knew. Although she tried to be supportive, she had little to say as well.

I decided to walk to the church and talk to my pastor, Bro. Veale. On the way there, I worried about what he would think of me, but I had to talk to someone. I told him everything, starting with the day I went with Verlon to the barracks. I told him about all of the horrible months of guilt and condemnation and how I thought God did not love me anymore and to top it off, I was now pregnant. He patiently listened to me talk and cry.

Bro. Veale did not condemn me or reject me. He was glad I trusted him enough to come and talk to him about such personal matters. With his kind and loving spirit, he reassured me that he loved me and didn't think any less of me. He read scriptures about God's love, forgiveness, and His promises to never leave me and that He was always with me. I felt much better, and I wished I had not taken so long to talk to him.

A couple of days after we got the news that I was pregnant, my father came home from work in the middle of the afternoon. He called me and my mother to the den away from the rest of the family. I was glad to have him say something to me, anything. He had not spoken to me since the day he found out I was pregnant. It was very obvious he was still extremely upset. He emphatically stated, "No daughter of mine will be living under my roof pregnant!"

I don't know what I was expecting. I did know, and I certainly wasn't expecting him to say those words.

He stated I had two choices. The first choice was to leave his house. The second choice was to get rid of the baby. He then reiterated his earlier statement that no daughter of his would live in his house pregnant out of wedlock. I didn't know what to say or do. I just started crying like I always did. Without a word, my mother came over and put her arms around me. A little later that evening, I could hear my parents arguing about it in their bedroom. I could hear my mother begging him to let me have the baby. They could raise it as their child.

Unexpectedly, there was a knock at the front door. I answered it, and to my surprise, it was Verlon. I wasn't sure how to respond to him. I had not talked to him since the day he came up to the school and walked right by me as he focused his attention on another girl. My heart skipped a beat when I saw him. I had mixed emotions. Part of me was glad to see him, and part of me hated him at the same time. I had confided in one of my girlfriends about the pregnancy. She knew I had not told him about the pregnancy. I figured she must have told him.

My father came to the door and told Verlon to come in and for both of us to have a seat. It quickly became apparent that my father had called Verlon and asked him to come over. My dad didn't waste any time. He asked Verlon if he knew I was pregnant and then asked him what he planned on doing about it. I thought to myself, "How did he know it was Verlon?" I don't remember my father asking me who the father was, and I don't remember ever saying who the father was.

Looking back, I realize that we don't give our parents enough credit for what they know. They always seem to know far more than we imagined. Verlon told my father he did not know I was pregnant, and then he reached for my hand and held it. He told my dad he would stand by me. My father asked me to leave the room because he wanted to talk to Verlon alone. I don't know what my father said to him, but when I was called back into the room, my mother and father left. Verlon and I walked outside and stood in silence for a few minutes, not really knowing what to say to each other. He then made a statement that led me to believe he wasn't sure if he was the father. He grabbed my hand again and kissed me on my forehead telling me not to worry, that he was going to be there for me.

I wanted to believe he really cared for me but deep down inside, I knew he didn't. He had already showed me his true colors, and I didn't trust him. My father came back outside and told Verlon he would expect to find out his decision in the next couple of days and demanded that I come back in the house. A few days later, Verlon did call me. However, after that phone call, it would be many years before I would hear from him again. I often wondered if my father had anything to do with that. I found out from my friend he had gotten transferred to another base out of the state.

I woke up the next day thinking about the two choices my father had given me. After all, I was only fourteen years old and a freshman in high school. What was I going to do? If he put me out, where was I going to go? Although I was asked to make a choice, the choice was made for me. Two days after my father told me I had some choices to make, I was taken to the hospital. After I was examined, my parents were asked to come into the doctor's office, and I was asked to step out. I couldn't hear everything being said, but I heard the doctor say, "She is almost five months. We will have to hurry." I thought, *What is it they have to hurry and do?*

The next day, my mother told me I would not be going to school but to the hospital. I overheard her pleading with my father again about them raising the baby. My father did not come with us to the clinic. I thought I just had another doctor's appointment. Instead, when we arrived I was ushered immediately into a room and asked to take off my clothes and put on a gown. The nurse was very cold and rude. She started an IV and gave me a shot. Then, I was wheeled to a bed.

My mother was there, accompanied by my aunt who had come to the hospital with us. The nurse told my mother, "It will take a couple of hours." I was upset because no one talked to me, no one told me what was going on, and the nurse I had was just downright mean.

I had no idea what the shot was for or why I had an IV. My mother kept crying, and when I finally realized what was going on, I began crying as well. After about an hour, I started moaning because I was cramping very badly. When the nurse came in to check on me, she angrily said, "I bet you won't open your legs again. This will teach you a lesson to keep them closed!" Time progressed and so did the pain.

Finally, two nurses came into the room. One of the nurses had a trash bag in her hand and came to stand at the end of the bed. The other one put two pillows on top of me and kept pushing me down because I kept trying to sit up to see what they were doing. She began to press down hard on my stomach. The other nurse opened the trash bag and came closer to me. The memory of everything that happened is very vivid in my mind. At one point, the nurse pushed so hard I screamed from the pain. Then, I heard them whisper, "It's twins!" My mother aloud saying, "Oh no! It's twins!"

She got up and ran out of the room crying (she had been sitting at the end of the bed and could see everything that was happening). At that point, I forced myself up so I could see what was happening. Even though the nurse continued pushing me back down, I saw something go into the trash bag. Then the nurse tied the bag and walked out of the room. Just like that, it was all over. I was numb. Everything was hazy from that point. I don't even remember leaving the clinic.

I do remember how rude and mean the nurses were to me. I was not able to put my mother's words out of my mind when she said, "Oh no, it's twins!" I was also unable to escape the memory of the nurse who tied up the trash bag and walked out of the room. I eventually found out that my father had taken the time to search for a doctor that would do an abortion by inducing my labor so that I would deliver too soon for the babies to survive.

Let me state here I do not advocate abortion. The Bible tells us that He knew us before we were in our mother's womb. The psalmist goes on to say He shaped us and knew all of our members before we were born. If you are someone who has had an abortion and have been suffering from guilt and shame, don't allow your past to haunt you. Ask God to forgive you and receive His forgiveness. Ask Him to heal you from any emotional pain you may still be experiencing as a result of that past decision.

Know that God loves you with an everlasting love and does not condemn you. He has a plan and purpose for your life. I have had many opportunities to share my testimony with other women regarding this experience and have met women who are still hurting from their decision to abort their baby. I've been privileged to minister to some of these women and I've seen them healed and delivered. You can experience that same healing and deliverance.

Months went by. I had become very depressed. If a baby commercial came on while I was watching TV, I would start crying. I could not stand to see anything that had to do with a baby. I had tried to hide my feelings of depression and hoped no one saw my tears while we were sitting around watching TV. I didn't understand my feelings. Part of me thought I should be happy my life was back to normal again. The other part of me ached for the babies I would never know.

My mother knew and understood. I had not shared what I was going through with her, but she could always look at me and tell whether I was glad, mad, or sad. One day, she sat me down and lovingly explained to me that it did not matter how young I was. I had gotten pregnant, and therefore, my body was longing to hold the child I would have delivered.

It was now January, the month the babies would have been born. I went to bed that night low in spirit. I woke up during the night weeping. At first, I thought I was dreaming. Since then I've often thought it was a vision, but regardless of what it was, it was very real to me.

I heard someone tap on my bedroom door and then open it. I sat up to see who it was. My youth director, Rita Webb said, "I brought someone to see you." I looked to see who it was. It was Jesus! I couldn't see the details of His face because there was such a brightness surrounding Him, but I knew it was Jesus! He came over to me and sat on the bed and took my hand. He told me to stop crying and that everything was going to be alright.

The love and peace I felt emanating from Him was overwhelming. That night, all the sadness left me. I woke up the next morning with such joy in my heart! I am reminded of a scripture I had heard at my grandfather's funeral. Psalm 30:5 (KJV) says, "Weeping may endure for a night but joy comes in the morning."

Chapter 6

The Pink Angel

It was the winter of 1972. By this time, I was a sophomore in high school. There was a flu epidemic all over San Antonio. Not only were students sick but the teachers were getting sick as well. The schools shut down for a whole week. Everyone in my family got the flu at the same time. We were all bedridden, including my parents.

My baby sister Felicia Jo had a real bad case of it and stayed sick for two or three weeks. Because her fever would not break, mother took her to the doctor. The doctor told her my sister just had a bad case of the flu. Though she eventually got over the worst of it, she kept a low grade fever and constantly complained that her ear hurt. My mother took her back to the doctor a couple of times, but they always said her throat, chest and ears were fine, and there was no evidence of an infection.

One doctor stated Felicia was probably "faking it" and was just trying to get attention. She didn't need to try to get attention. One thing that was not lacking in our home was love and attention. Felicia started falling down and tripping over everything, she began bumping into walls. All of a sudden, she seemed to be really clumsy. I remember her teacher sent a note home about how messy her handwriting had gotten and that she would be sending home extra handwriting assignments for her. Even with practice and extra homework, her handwriting was still sloppy. My parents began to wonder if something was wrong.

One evening at the dinner table, Felicia knocked over her Kool-Aid and couldn't pick up her food without dropping it. When she got up from the table, she tripped and fell. Then she asked could she go outside to play, but in trying to go out the door, she kept hitting the wall. It was as if she could not see the door. She hit the wall so hard, she busted her forehead. Then my mother hysterically began saying, "Something is wrong with my baby, I don't care what the doctors say." Mom insisted they should take her to the emergency room right away. She kept saying I'm not leaving until they find out what is wrong with her.

My mother who was usually very kind and soft-spoken, created a scene in the emergency room. My father pleaded with them to admit Felicia, if for no other reason but to calm his wife down. The doctors didn't think they would find anything wrong but agreed to the admission and to run some test just to give my mother peace of mind. The first set of test came back negative, but my mother wasn't satisfied with that and insisted there was something wrong. The second set of test still showed negative results.

Then they decided there was something wrong with her eyes so they called in an ophthalmologist. He found that one muscle in her eye was too short and as a result, it was causing her to see double. This explained why she had become so clumsy. The doctor suggested eye surgery, but again, my mother was not satisfied and continued insisting there was something else wrong with her baby.

The Pink Angel

She begged the doctor to keep looking. He told her "Okay, Mrs. Hornsby, there is one more test I can run—a spinal tap, but it's dangerous." She promised if that test came back negative she would agree to the eye surgery. They also took a CT scan of the brain.

The same doctor that told my mother Felicia was "faking" and just trying to "get attention" was her attending physician in the hospital. Now that same physician had to give my mother the test results. Felicia had an inoperable malignant tumor at the base of her brain. Though doctors suggested cobalt treatment, they did not offer much hope that this would be the cure they needed. The tumor was pressing on an area that was causing the ear to hurt, the double vision, and all the clumsiness. My parents were heartbroken. A mother's intuition is amazing.

My mother would not give up and kept insisting that she knew there was something wrong with her daughter. There were six of us, and my mother was in tuned to each one of us. She always had the ability to take one look at me and tell if I was sick or upset. Later in life, when I became an adult, I would call her. If something was going on with me, inevitably she seemed to always know and would ask me what was wrong.

The cobalt treatments started right away. Felicia was to remain in the hospital the duration of the treatments due to the severity of the side effects. She lost her hair and got very bloated. The treatments made her very sick. After seeing how hard the treatments were on Felicia, my mother started taking her to the chapel before going to treatment. They would pray together, asking the Lord to take away the side effects. The nausea subsided. This was amazing to the doctors, and the day finally came for her to be released from the hospital.

Felicia Jo was six years old. She was always laughing and full of joy. We could never tell whether she was scared, in pain, or just what she was feeling. Felicia never complained. She was a lot like my mother: gentle, kind, and sweet. She loved telling jokes and was just happy by nature.

About four months after getting out of the hospital, the clumsiness started again. She was having difficulty walking, and her speech was beginning to slur. The tumor was growing. The doctors said there was nothing they could do. They told my parents the cancer was going to ravish through her body quickly and suggested she be admitted back into the hospital and kept there until she died. My parents were adamant that leaving her in the hospital until she died was not an option. My mother said she would take her home, and our love would keep her alive as long as possible. Her limbs would become more difficult for her to use until she could not move them at all.

One Sunday at church, as the pastor was giving the invitation at the end of his sermon for those who wanted to accept Jesus Christ as their savior, Felicia got up and went forward. By this time, one of her legs was almost completely paralyzed. The walk to the altar took her a long time. She finally made it to the altar. Bro. Veale asked her why she had come, and with slurred speech she told him she wanted to give her life to Jesus and she wanted to get baptized. No one had prompted her. She made this decision on her own. An elderly man got up and came to the altar. Tearfully, he said if this little girl who can barely walk can come and give her life to Jesus, he could, too. This started a chain reaction. That day, about eight to ten people came to the altar to give their lives to Christ.

Every day after that, Felicia wanted me to read the Bible to her and pray with her. She loved the Lord. There were times I felt sad and afraid she would die. The Lord would speak to me in a still, small voice, telling me to be at peace and to keep my eyes on Him and reassuring me He was in control.

One day, a family friend came to visit Felicia and gave her some money. The friend told her to get herself something special with it. My mother asked her later what she wanted to buy with her money. She told her she wanted to have a party, and she wanted to use the money to buy the food for it. My mother was surprised at this and asked her whether she wouldn't rather go to the toy store and buy a new doll. Felicia told my mother she wanted to buy chips, sodas, cookies, and sandwich meat because she was giving us a party.

In our home, my father always said the prayer before we ate. The day of the party when it was time to eat, my dad started to pray, but my sister stopped him and said she was giving the party so she wanted to pray. She took her time and prayed for each one of us individually, calling each of us by name. She had so much love in her heart. We were all amazed. Everyone had tears in their eyes, especially my mother who had to leave the room to keep from letting Felicia know she was crying.

Felicia's illness progressed steadily overtime. Eventually total paralysis set in until the only thing that she could move was her eyes. My mother kept her at home as long as possible until her breathing became too labored, and she had to be admitted into the hospital. The doctors told my parents she only had about three days to live. Though we were all saddened by the news, we took comfort in something else they told us. They said Felicia would not have survived as long as she had without the love and support she was given at home. It had been a year since they suggested we leave her in the hospital until her death. Three days after Felicia had been re-admitted into the hospital, my sister Kathy and I were in a school play. I was supposed to go to the hospital after the cast party, so I could spend the night with her. Soon after arriving at the cast party, Kathy felt an urgency for us to hurry home. When we arrived, there was a dark cloud hanging over our house. The atmosphere surrounding our home intimated the news that my sister was gone.

It had been three days, just as the doctor had predicted. My grandmother, who we called Granny, was with Felicia when she passed away. Granny told us while she was with Felicia, she woke up out of her comatose state. She shared with us Felicia showed no signs of being afraid or of being in pain. She simply opened her eyes, smiled at her, and then she was gone.

For several hours after hearing the news, I was just numb. We stayed up most of the night, but by daybreak the reality of what was going on and the pain of our loss had set in. The next day the youth group at my church had a paper drive scheduled. I wasn't sure about going, but my mother encouraged me to go ahead and participate in it. It was only by God's grace I was able to get through it without falling apart.

My parents picked out a pink brocade casket. It was beautiful. Felicia was dressed in a pink ruffled dress with pink and white ribbons in her hair. She looked so beautiful, like a little pink angel. On the funeral program above her picture was written: "The Pink Angel."

We buried Felicia the week of her seventh birthday. During the funeral service, my heart felt like it was going to break into a million pieces. I just could not stop crying.

All of a sudden, I felt a soft breeze wafting over me. It was the feeling I got from the warm oil again! I felt the peace of God fill my soul once more. I no longer felt the need to cry. I was at peace, and I even felt a sense of joy. I knew she was in heaven, and that thought alone gave me a lot of assurance. Even though Felicia was with us only a short time, she was truly a blessing to our lives.

Chapter 7

His Healing and Power of Protection

"*B*y His stripes are you healed." This scripture in 1 Peter 2:24 was one I was going to have to stand on for my life in the months ahead. We buried my sister, Felicia on January 26, 1973. The Lord had sustained me through my first encounter with the death of an immediate family member. I was learning to lean on Jesus more and more. He was teaching me to keep my eyes on him and to trust him with every situation I faced in my life.

Just three months after the passing of my sister, my parents would be faced with another crisis. For about six months prior to this, I had been feeling sharp needle-like pains in my left hip that would come and go. My mother had her hands full taking care of my sister, so I decided not to bother her with it and paid little attention to the pain.

However, the pain became increasingly severe, and it came more often. Finally, I broke down and told my mother, and she took me to the doctor. He said he thought I had probably pulled a muscle, and when it didn't get any better we went back. That doctor told me it was "just growing pains." Every time we went to Wilford Hall

Medical Center on Lackland Air Force Base, we saw a different doctor.

About three months after my sister died, the pain had gotten so bad I could hardly stand it. When we went back to the doctor this time, I spoke up, telling the doctor about my sister and how one doctor had told my mother she was "just trying to get attention" and later that same doctor told us she had cancer and now she was dead. I demanded that he run some tests and find out what was wrong with my hip. I surprised myself. He looked at me and said, "Yes, ma'am, I'll get on that right away." After he examined me, he sent me for an X-ray.

A mass was found in my left hip area that they were going to have to remove it and then send the tumor off to the lab for testing in order to determine if it was malignant or benign. The night before surgery, I was nervous and afraid. As I was tearfully praying, I heard the Lord gently say to me, "Hush my child. Don't cry, I'm standing right here by your side." I actually sensed Him come and sit on my bed and whisper these words to me. When it was time for me to be taken to the operating room, I was no longer afraid.

In these days and times when surgery is scheduled, more often than not, you go home the same day, but back in 1973, you stayed in the hospital at least five days. I had to stay in the hospital until the test results came back from the laboratory. That took about three weeks.

In the meantime, I spent a lot of time reading my Bible to pass time while I was in the hospital. One day I read a scripture in the book of 1 Peter about healing. I was so excited! Something exploded in me as I read "Who his own self bare our sins in his own body on the tree that we being dead to sins, should live unto righteousness: by whose stripes ye were healed." *by whose stripes you were healed"* (KJV)!

It seemed as though those words leaped right off the page and into my spirit. I decided at that very moment that I was already healed. I just needed to believe it.

The day finally came for the doctors to give us the test results. I determined in my heart that if it was bad news, I was going to take God at His Word and believe that I was healed. I called my mother and told her of the stand I was taking, that no matter what the doctors told us, God was going to heal me. I didn't want her to even come up there if she wasn't going to have faith with me for healing. I said, "Mom, I want you to be strong; promise me if it is bad news, you won't fall apart." For some reason I just knew we were going to have to have unwavering faith when we went into the doctor's office. I wasn't afraid of the results, but I think I knew the test results were not going to be normal.

My mother was still so broken up over the loss of my sister that when the doctor told her it was a tumor and could be cancerous; she broke down and cried and cried. It was about 3 p.m. when the nurse came to take me and my mother down to the doctor's office. When we walked in, he had somewhat of a grim look on his face and seemed nervous as he made small talk. Finally, he told us the results showed the tumor to be malignant. I had fibrosarcoma, a type of cancer that affects the soft connective tissues in the body. The doctor said I would need another operation, explaining they needed to go back in and remove two and half muscles in my left hip area to make sure they remove all of the cancer. He went on to explain, as a result of removing the necessary muscles, I would probably walk with a limp the rest of my life, and I would not be able to run or dance again. In addition, this type of cancer had the ability to resurface again. I squeezed my mother's hand, more concerned about her than I was about me. She loved her children very much and would often tell us we were her life.

Nevertheless, she was a trooper and didn't shed a single tear. I boldly told the doctor I was a Christian, and Jesus was Lord of my life and God had promised me in his Word that I would be healed. I said to him, "You watch and see; God is going to heal me!" I had no fear as we walked out of his office that day. I remained in his perfect peace. My heart was fixed, and my mind was made up.

While in the hospital I always had lots of visitors: teachers, classmates, family members, and my pastor who came almost every day. The youth group at Marbach Christian Church was on fire for the Lord. We were very close and supportive of one another. We prayed about everything together. During this tough time, their visits to the hospital were a real encouragement to me. When they came to visit, we would go throughout the halls singing Christian songs and visiting other patients, asking them if they wanted prayer. I had a lot of time on my hands.

I had to wait almost two weeks before we could proceed with the second surgery. During my hospital stay, I read the Bible and listened to Christian music. One of the scriptures that really helped me during that time was Romans 8:28 (KJV): "And we know that all things work together for good to them that love God, to them who are the called according to His purpose."

This scripture helped me to realize that the Lord can take any problem or situation and use it to work for my good and His glory. I understood the sickness did not come from Him, but somehow good was going to come from it and He would get the glory for it.

One of my favorite Christian artists at that time was Andre Crouch. One of his most popular songs was entitled "Through It All." Some of the lyrics were: "Through it all, I've learned to trust in Jesus. Through it all I've learned to depend upon His Word. I thank God for my problems, for if I never had a problem, I'd never know God could solve them." I listened to this song just before going into surgery. It helped to reassure me that God was in control.

When I woke up, I was in excruciating pain and had to be heavily sedated for hours at a time. I suffered awful muscle spasms. I also had trouble with my memory as I could not remember who or if anyone had been to see me. I asked my friend Teresa and my sister Kathy why they had not been to see me on the day of my surgery. I actually thought it had been just a day since the surgery when actually a week had passed by.

Both of them had been there every day for a week, but I was so heavily sedated I wasn't aware of their presence. They told me I woke up a couple of times to talk to them. I had no recollection of talking to anyone. I later found out I was given too much anesthesia, and it was affecting my memory. I had trouble spelling and remembering certain facts, but eventually the effects of the anesthesia wore off. The next few weeks were filled with hours of painful physical therapy. I had to learn how to walk all over again.

In June of 1973, after four long months, the day finally came for me to be released from the hospital. I was on crutches and was going to have them for three months. Afterwards, I would have to use a cane for a little while. I was sent home with a prescription of muscle relaxers and told I would have muscle spasms off and on for a period of time until the remaining muscles in my leg became used to working harder to make up for the muscles that were missing.

The doctor reminded my parents I would have a limp the rest of my life and that the cancer could return in three years. If it came back, it would either come back in the same area or in my breast. I reminded the doctor and my parents that I was healed, and I was not expecting the cancer to come back. I told the doctor, "When I come back to see you for my follow-up appointment, I won't be on crutches or using a cane."

The same day I returned home, when I walked in the house I said to myself, *If I'm healed I don't need these crutches*. I laid the crutches down and walked from the front door to the back door two or three times without my crutches. My mother was having a fit, insisting I use the crutches. I was praising God, saying, "See, Mom, I told you. I am walking, and there is no limp. I jumped up and down and ran through the house. I took the crutches and threw them in the back yard. I really thought my mother was going to faint. She was afraid I was going to hurt myself. I have to admit the next day, I was a bit sore. My mother insisted that at the very least, I use the cane.

It was the end of June and almost time for Christian Family Camp. The thought of missing camp made me more determined to be completely recovered as soon as possible. At my two week follow-up appointment, I walked in my doctor's office on a cane and not the crutches. He couldn't believe it and was upset I was using the cane and not the crutches. He said I needed to use the crutches at least three more months and then graduate to the cane. I told him when I came back for the next appointment I wouldn't be using the cane, either.

I went to camp against the doctor's advice. According to him, I needed three full months for recovery, but according to the Word of God, I was already healed. My parents knew how much I loved going to camp. I begged them to let me go if I promised to take the cane and try to stay off my leg as much as possible. The lady who always sponsored me promised to keep an eye on me, and my friends promised they would not let me overdo it. Reluctantly, my parents finally agreed to let me go.

When we arrived, I was so excited about seeing my friends, I opened the car door almost before the car stopped. I jumped out and ran to hug my dear friend Sonya. My friend Teresa, who had been in the car with me, came running after me with the cane. She said, "Ava, do you realize what you just did? You ran without your cane, and you're not limping!" That was the last day I used my cane. There was no limp and no soreness.

When I got back from camp, it was time for another checkup. I walked into the doctor's office with no crutches, no cane, and most of all no limp! I jumped up and down. I reminded the doctor of what I told him during my last visit. God had completely healed me. Glory to God! Needless to say, the doctor couldn't believe it. I have been cancer free since then.

Chapter 8
A State of Depression

Satan comes to steal, kill, and destroy. He is a liar and a thief. His goal is to deceive you and take you down a road that leads only to destruction. The good news is, Satan is a defeated foe, and Jesus is Lord. The shed blood of Jesus Christ defeated Satan at the cross. God's Word says in Romans 8:37 (KJV), "You are more than a conqueror through Him who loved us." 1 John 4:4 (KJV) says, "Greater is He that is in you than he that is in the world."

I know that now and have since learned how to wage warfare against the enemy. In my senior year of high school, I fell prey to Satan's schemes and his attempt to destroy me. I loved the Lord, but I had not matured enough in my walk with God to recognize Satan's wicked devices or how to fight against them.

In the last chapter, I was up. In these next two chapters, I was down, but I still come out victorious as it is evident by the title of the book: Going *from Glory to Glory*.

It was 1974. I was now a senior in high school. Soon after school started, the counselor called me into the office to tell me I wasn't going to be able to graduate because I had not completed necessary assignments and tests during my junior year. I had spent four months in the hospital and worked on some of those assignments but had not finished them. This news upset me greatly.

The counselor promised to communicate with the district office to see if there was anything that could be done. They agreed to let me graduate if I could complete all missed tests and major assignments from my junior year with passing grades, along with the senior class work. It was going to be very difficult. However, I was determined to do it. I had a ton of homework and would have to spend several hours after school each night, trying to catch up.

Apart from the painful muscle spasms I would have from time to time, my health was good. When I was released from the hospital, the doctor told me I would have them for a while, but they would eventually go away. I was sent home with a long-term prescription for the muscle relaxers, Valium and Librium.

For some reason everything began to depress me. I didn't know why I was depressed, and no matter what I did, I could not shake it. There would be bouts of sadness that would just come over me, and I would start crying for no reason. Even though it had been three years since my pregnancy, painful memories about that started bombarding my mind again. I felt empty inside, and periodically, I'd cry. My arms would ache with longing for the twins I would never hold. I thought I had put all of that behind me. This was my senior year. I was very popular and held the position of first runner up for Homecoming Queen. Why wasn't I happy?

I was also having teenage problems of child versus parent. Remember those days when you felt like your parents were your worst enemies and you knew better than

A State Of Depression

they did? I've mentioned previously that my father was very strict. He wasn't mean, just strict. But at the time, I thought he was just being mean. After I got pregnant, it seemed like he was harder on me than he was on my other siblings. I couldn't get away with anything and was often accused of doing something I had not done.

Our football team had won their first victory over our chief rival who had beaten us three years in a row. There was such excitement about the game that school ended early that day. This was to be the game of all games. When we won, everyone went wild. The celebration on the field must have lasted for an hour. Parties were being held everywhere. Everyone from the youth group was at the game, and we all decided to go back to the church and celebrate and have a time of worship and a prayer meeting.

It was late when I got home. My oldest sister had gotten home before me. When I walked into the house, my father was waiting for me. He was very angry and immediately began to accuse me of being out with a boy. When I told him I had been at church with the youth group, he insisted I was lying. This had not been the first time he accused me of being somewhere with a boy. It was like I could not live down the fact that I had gotten pregnant. I was very hurt by the accusation especially since I had been at church. I could have been anywhere and thought he should be glad I was at church. Nevertheless, he had made it abundantly clear, he did not believe me. I went to bed feeling defeated.

I began to think maybe I should have been out drinking and partying like all my other classmates. These thoughts only served to add to my depression. Just a few days after the game, I had a Home Economics assignment that entailed having a dinner party and serving an Italian meal. My teacher had to attend so she could grade me. I invited a few friends to include my boyfriend Richard. We served wine with the meal since this was part of Italian cuisine. Afterwards, my boyfriend and I went out, and as we were leaving he saw there was a bottle of wine that had not been opened, so he grabbed it to take with us.

He said a little wine won't hurt anyone and why waste it. We picked up another couple and asked them to join us. While we were out, we ended up drinking the whole bottle of wine. Richard started feeling bad about drinking. We started arguing. He tried to blame me while I put the blame on him. For some reason my boyfriend got real angry about it and decided to take me home. The next day I called Richard to apologize about our argument, but his sister answered. She was yelling, "It's all your fault, if it had not been for you; this would not have happened!" She cussed me out and hung up the phone. I tried calling her back, but she would just hang up on me again.

I frantically called one of our friends who had been with us the night before to find out what had happened. I was told that Richard lost control of the car. He was thrown from the vehicle and had broken his back and both of his jaws. Neither of our two friends who were riding with him sustained any injuries. I asked if she could come get me and take me to the hospital right away.

Richard was a year or two older than me. He was white. We went to the same church. My parents didn't have a problem with him being white, but his family had a problem with me being black. His sister especially had a problem with it and made it known that she didn't like the fact her brother was dating a black girl.

When I got to the hospital, his sister lit into me again and tried to prevent me from going into Richard's room. She kept blaming me for the wreck, saying I was the one who talked him into drinking and that she heard about the argument we had, which upset her brother and ultimately caused him to lose control of the car. Surprisingly their mother told her to stop and let me come into the room. I wasn't prepared for what I saw. Richard had bruises all over his body and tubes were everywhere. He was in a great deal of pain. I was afraid he wouldn't want to see me, but he was glad to see me. I agreed with his sister and kept telling him it was my fault, and I was so sorry.

    The next day, I called to see how Richard was doing. His sister answered and was still very angry with me. She told me her family did not want me to come back to the hospital, and if I did come, I would not be permitted to see Richard and for me never to call their house again. The words "it was all your fault" kept ringing in my ears as I hung up the phone. All the other negative thoughts I had been having for the last couple of weeks started ringing in my ears, as well. My head was spinning and my mind was being bombarded with horrible thoughts.

    I was the only one home at the time. I was crying, and I kept telling myself everything has gone wrong. I felt so frazzled, and I wanted all the voices to stop. Suddenly something snapped inside of me. I went numb and like a zombie, I walked over to the medicine cabinet and got the bottle of Valium, the bottle of Librium, and the bottle of aspirin out and without forethought, I swallowed all of the Valium, all of the Librium, and a handful of aspirin.

    There must have been at least twenty pills of Valium and twenty pills of Librium, and I'm not sure how many aspirin I took. It was Tuesday, the night of our youth prayer meeting. I was able to get through dinner without showing any signs of what I had just done.

After about an hour into the meeting, it became obvious to my friend Teresa that something was wrong with me. She knew me pretty well and was aware I had been depressed lately and how upset I was about Richard's accident. She asked me what was wrong and told me I was acting funny. She pulled me out of the meeting, telling me to follow her to the bathroom. I told her nothing was wrong, but she was not convinced.

She asked me point blank if I had taken something or been drinking. She finally went and got the pastor, telling him something was wrong with me, and she suspected I had taken drugs or had been drinking. They questioned me, but after denying it a couple of times, I finally admitted that I had taken some pills but lied and told them all I had taken was a bunch of aspirin. I just couldn't bring myself to tell them I had taken over forty tranquilizers. I don't think they believed me because of the way I was acting.

Bro. Veale ran to get the car. In the meantime, I fell down the stairs. When I was finally able to get back up, I stumbled outside where I tripped and fell again. As I hit the cement, I remember saying, "Lord, I don't want to die. I've made such a mess of everything; can you fix it?"

My pastor took me home. He told my parents he had called and spoke to a nurse at the hospital and told them I had taken a handful of aspirin and she recommended I force myself to throw up and for them to give me a strong cup of coffee.

My parents were frantic. My mother was crying, and my dad was fussing. He did not know whether to take me to the hospital or put me to bed. He kept yelling, "How could you do this? What's wrong with you?" I hated the fact that he was yelling at me. I walked in the bathroom and grabbed a bottle of green rubbing alcohol and began drinking it. My mother walked in just before I finished the bottle.

My dad settled down and asked me if I wanted to go to the hospital, but I told him no, I just wanted to go to bed. As I was dozing off to sleep, the reality of what I had done was setting in, and I was afraid I was going to die. I prayed again, telling the Lord I had made a mess of everything and that I didn't really want to die. I asked Him again if He could straighten out the mess and to please allow me to live. My mother sat by my side all night. I could hear her praying for me off and on all night.

I woke up bright and early the next morning just as I had done every other morning. I got up, showered, got dressed and went to school. I could still feel the effects of all the pills I had taken, but I was able to function—or so I thought. After lunch, I passed out cold and was rushed to the hospital in an ambulance. The doctor ran tests, and when the toxicology report came back, the doctor told my parents that I should be dead or in a coma. He kept stating it was a miracle that I was alive. I was in and out but was able to tell them how many pills I had actually taken the night before. They felt it would do no good to pump my stomach at that point, but they pumped it anyway just to satisfy my parents, so they would feel like they were doing something for me.

The doctor gave my parents the choice of putting me in the hospital or taking me home. They chose to take me home. A few days later, I was admitted to a hospital for teenagers with emotional and behavioral problems. Even though I knew in the back of my mind that the Lord had saved my life, I was still depressed and seemed to be angry with everyone. I wasn't sure why I was so angry. Satan was doing a number on me.

My mother brought my Bible to me, along with some other items. I put the Bible up and didn't read it for several days until one day I felt drawn to it like a magnet. I finally picked it up and thumbed through the pages until it fell open to a story about the apostle Paul. He had been bitten by a snake. The snake must have been very deadly because the scripture says that everyone present expected Paul to swell up and suddenly drop dead, but he didn't.

The scripture said Paul suffered no harm. When I read those words "suffered no harm," I heard a voice coming through the loud speaker "Ava, You are my child, and no harm shall come to you. I love you." I had a flashback of all the pills I swallowed. I looked around to see if anyone else was in the room, but I was alone. I was sure the voice had come through the loud speaker. I heard it again loud and clear. I recognized the voice of my Heavenly Father.

Suddenly, all of the anger, the depression, and the sadness just melted away. I began to weep, but the tears were tears of joy. Whatever had been oppressing me was gone. As I was crying, I could sense my inner man rising up inside of me. I decided right at that moment I would not allow anything to depress me so much that it would cause me to want to take my life. I wanted to live. I asked the Lord to forgive me for trying to take my life and thanked him for allowing me to live.

The psychologist had an exit interview with my parents when I was being discharged. He told them he didn't think I had any major problems but felt strongly the prescription of Valium and Librium for the muscle spasms caused the depression. He shared with them I had been taking the tranquilizers to help me sleep without their knowledge, and depression was a side effect of that type of medication.

Satan's plan was to stop God's purpose for my life. He had laid a trap, using the tranquilizers as the bait. The trap was convincing me that the pills would help me sleep, knowing depression would be the side effect and depression would lead to my death. Oh, but God had a plan for my life! The Word of God says the purposes of God shall prevail, and most importantly, what really spoiled Satan's plan were my mother's prayers. She sat by my bedside, praying all night. Praise God!

I am so glad Jesus allowed me to live. It was a miracle. John 10:10 (NKJV) says "The thief does not come except to steal, and to kill, and to destroy; I have come that they may have life and that they may have it more abundantly."

If you are suffering from depression and are having thoughts of taking your life, find someone who will pray for you and encourage you. Cry out to Jesus and ask Him to help you. Choose to live. Know that God loves you and He has a purpose for your life. Jeremiah 29:11(NIV) states "For I know the plans I have for you, declares the Lord, plans to prosper you and not to harm you, plans to give you hope and a future."

Chapter 9

A Broken Dream

*H*e was tall, dark and handsome. His name was Tim Wade. He was a singer and piano player in a Christian group called the Hope of Glory. Before I met him, a friend of mine, who also sang in the Hope of Glory, wrote me to let me know they were coming to San Antonio and would be doing a concert at our church. She teased me in the letter that she had met my husband, and she just knew we would hit it off right away and that we would be just right for each other.

When we were introduced to one another, it was awkward because they had told him about me and me about him. My first thoughts were no, he's too shy for me. They stayed in San Antonio for a while before traveling to some of the surrounding cities. I followed them to as many concerts as I could. Whenever the group had some down time, Tim would come and visit. Before long, we were talking marriage.

I was so excited! I imagined how we would travel and be in ministry together. Wow! I could hardly wait. When I told my parents I was getting married, they were not excited at all. As a matter of fact, they didn't even respond. My plans were not lining up with their plans. I was a freshman in college, and their plan was to see me graduate. However, I thought every girl's dream was to find her Prince Charming, get married, and live happily ever after. At least I grew up believing that was every girl's dream. I would try to talk to my parents about wedding plans, but they weren't taking me seriously.

Tim and I made plans to go to Georgia for two weeks, so I could meet his family. My mother promised me when we got back, if we still wanted to get married, she would take me to look at wedding dresses and we could start making plans. Tim's family was excited about the engagement. We picked a date while we were there. I got along well with his mother. We had a wonderful time and came back more in love than we were when we left. We prayed together, asking the Lord to direct our footsteps as we wanted His will to be done in our lives, and if this was not His will, we asked Him to show us. We both felt God was confirming to us we were on the right track and came back very excited about the wedding.

Tim was on the road quite a bit, and I began to grow weary as it was difficult to sustain a close relationship with someone who was on the road most of the time. There were no cell phones back then and the phone calls were few and far between when he was on the road. Although he wrote often, I was only able to see him once or twice a month.

Sometimes it was only at one of his concerts and that didn't give us much time together. We had picked our wedding date, but we hadn't done much planning. I complained one night to him after one of his concerts that we never had time to talk about the wedding, and I wasn't sure he really wanted to get married. It was six months before our wedding date, and we had not finalized any details.

His response was for me to call his mother and talk to her about it and whatever my parents and I wanted would be okay with him. He assured me he loved me and still wanted to get married. He promised he would have some down time soon, and we would finalize all the plans then.

A couple of weeks later, Tim called to invite me to come to Houston for the weekend. They weren't having a concert, and I would have him all to myself. I was a little disappointed when I got there because I was hoping he was going to tell me they were going to be off for a month or so, but he had to get right back on the road on Monday. We had a great time, though. When Sunday came, we both hated that we didn't have more time to spend with each other.

While driving to the bus terminal, Tim was quiet and seemed deep in thought. When we got there we hugged each other over and over telling each other, "I love you" and "I'm going to miss you." Then it was time to get on the bus. Tim walked me to the door of the bus. Everyone had gotten on the bus except me.

While holding my hand and kissing me and acting as if he did not want me to leave, out of the blue he said, "Look, Ava, this is just not going to work." I looked confused and said, "What's not going to work?" The bus driver looked at us and said, "Ma'am, we have to go."

My heart skipped a beat, and I wasn't sure I understood what Tim was saying or I didn't want to understand what he was saying. I begged the driver to give me a few more seconds. Without waiting for the driver to answer me, I asked Tim, "What are you talking about?" He just made hand motions pointing to me and then to him and said, "It's just not going to work."

The bus driver said, "Lady, I have to close the door, and we have to go." Tim stood there looking at me. Then he dropped his head and walked away. I was stunned! I felt like someone had just kicked me in my stomach. I didn't know whether to cry, scream, or kick someone.

I got on the bus and slowly found a seat. *Wait a minute, I thought to myself, I'm confused, after the romantic weekend we just had, confessing our love for each other as we held hands. He waits until the bus is about to leave before telling me it's not going to work*! Part of me wanted to stop the bus and run after him and choke him, and the other part of me wanted to run after him and say, "But you told me just this morning you loved me, and we finally talked about the wedding."

On the ride back to San Antonio, I sat there numb. I didn't cry, I didn't even move. I just sat there in shock.

For the next few days I walked around our house like a zombie. My mother later told me she would say something to me, and I wouldn't even respond to her or anyone else. I was going to San Antonio Junior College at the time. I was in the middle of my psychology class when the numbness wore off, and I finally broke. I burst out crying right in the middle of class. It felt like someone cut me up with a sharp knife. I was so mad that it hurt, and I certainly didn't want to cry. I wanted Tim to be the one hurting and crying, not me. I cried for days and avoided everyone as much as possible. I did not want anyone to know why I was crying.

I started drinking. I had convinced myself I needed to stay numb. As soon as I got home from class, I would walk straight to my father's bar that he kept stocked and gulped down whatever was open straight from the bottle. I didn't want anyone to know about it, so I did it quickly, hoping no one would see me. I started doing this before I went to class, after I came from class, and just before I went to bed. I wasn't spending much time in prayer. I decided it was God's fault my dream was not coming true. I wanted to know why he allowed my heart to be broken. I felt stupid, embarrassed, and deep down inside, I knew my parents believed we had rushed into something that wasn't going to work, and that is why they never wanted to discuss the wedding. Remember when Tim and I came back from visiting his parents, we were so in love with each other?

I mentioned earlier how we prayed together asking for God's perfect will to be done in our lives. I assumed surely it was part of God's will. We were in love, and we were getting married. God did answer our prayer. That's why this was happening. We prayed for His will to be done as we made our plans. If I had stopped for a minute and really listened to the Lord, I might have heard Him say, "I have other plans for you." To be honest, I probably would not have listened at the time. My heart and mind were not open to receive God's plan. If it were different from my own plans, I would not have heard it.

I now believe, I was in love with the idea of being in love and wanted to have what I believed was the dream of every little girl. That dream entailed that I would grow up, get swept off my feet by my Prince Charming, get married, and live happily ever after. It's not always the fault of someone else or the devil that we suffer heartache and pain. Some of the things we go through are brought on by our own stubborn ways and the choices we make. There are many promises in the Word of God, but there is not one that says you will never have trials and tribulations. There is nothing that says your heart won't ever be broken.

Sometimes God uses these things, or allows them to shape and mold us into the person He wants us to be. He will order our steps and direct our path toward the open doors He wants us to walk through.

It was almost Christmas and though it had been months, I was hoping maybe Tim would call or send a card or something. I had a dream one night that I was doubled over in pain and had to be rushed to the hospital. Part of my dream was about me being aware that I was going in the wrong direction, and I was backsliding from the Lord. It was like there was a strong force pulling me like a magnet away from God. When I woke up from the dream, it stayed on my mind all day. A week later, while out shopping for Christmas presents, I was suddenly doubled over in severe sharp pains in my pelvic area.

My mother rushed me over to the walk-in clinic on Lackland Air Force Base, and the doctor that saw me sent me to the GYN clinic that same day. That doctor said he thought the pain was due to double ovulation and for me to come back the next month after my next menstrual cycle when he would put me on birth control pills to regulate it. The next day was Christmas Eve, but again while out shopping, the pain hit me hard. It was so excruciating, I was crawling on the floor in tears.

Once again, we went back to the emergency room, only to be told since I had seen a doctor earlier at the GYN clinic and was told it had something to do with my menstrual cycle, the only thing they could do is give me something for the pain. They didn't even examine me.

When I woke up the next morning, my temperature was 104, and I was bleeding. I had already had my menstrual cycle for that month, so we weren't sure what was happening. My father called the hospital this time instead of taking me. He was advised to just wait until after the holidays, and I was given an appointment for January 2 at 8 a.m.

My dad was so frustrated and upset. The pain pills weren't helping much. I can remember him coming in my room with a tall glass of something from his bar. I think it was Scotch. My mom was protesting, but he insisted and told me to drink it straight up until it was all gone. He said "We have to do something, I can't stand seeing her in pain like this." I turned the glass up and drank it all as my father had instructed me. I remember falling back and passing out. When I finally woke up, I had missed Christmas and slept straight through until the following day. Since I was in so much pain, it seemed to take forever for that day to come but, finally, it was January 2.

As soon as the doctor examined me, he was furious and wanted the name of the doctor who saw me the first time. On the military bases, every time you go to the clinic, you are going to see a different doctor. I was glad I had this particular doctor on that day. He was especially angry with the emergency room doctor who didn't examine me. The doctor promised my mother he was going to do something about it. He found my uterus to be full of blood and thought he felt a large mass. He told me and my parents I was hemorrhaging and was going to have to have emergency surgery and that I needed to leave the clinic and go straight to the hospital.

While I was being prepared to go into surgery, my backslidden state was ever before me. I hadn't prayed in weeks. I had been mad at God, but now I needed to pray. I wanted to pray, but I felt guilty and was ashamed of myself for being mad at God. I remembered the dream I had weeks

A Broken Dream

earlier. In the dream, I was doubled over in pain and was aware something was pulling me away from the Lord.

I was afraid and didn't want to go into surgery without the assurance that everything was going to be okay. I said, "Lord, I can't pray for myself but would you put me on someone else's heart, so they will pray for me?" The Lord answered swiftly. My mother had rushed home to pack a suitcase for me and while she was there, someone called her and said, "I've been thinking about Ava all morning. Is she okay? The Holy Spirit just prompted me to start praying for her." My mother gave her the details, and she agreed to call the prayer chain at church and get them to praying for me as well.

I had to be examined by a team of doctors who had been assigned to me. All eight doctors agreed there was a mass about the size of a grapefruit and that it was a strong possibility I would have to have a hysterectomy. That was not good news to a nineteen-year-old woman. I wanted to have children.

I was taken into surgery, but by the time the doctors opened me up, the grapefruit-sized mass had disappeared, and all they found was a ruptured cyst. There was no tumor, no malignancy, and most of all, I didn't have to have a hysterectomy.

The doctor asked my mother, if I spoke a foreign language? She told them no and that I had never taken a language in school. He told her "That's funny because the whole time we were operating on her, she was talking in a foreign language, and then in English, she prayed for each doctor by name." With the exception of the head doctor, I didn't know the names of the team of doctors in the operating room with me that day.

When my mother told me what the doctor said, I began to weep, not because I was sad but because Jesus had come through for me again. I forsook him, yet He remained faithful and true to His Word. He didn't forsake me! How great is His faithfulness! When a child of God cries out to the Lord (Adonai), he hears them and answers them.

The Great Physician, Jehovah Rapha (our healer), had prevailed once again on my behalf. I would later give birth to three wonderful children.

Someone called Tim and told him I was in the hospital. The day I was being released, he showed up at the hospital. He told my mother he didn't want her to do anything and He was going to take care of me for the next few days. I was so groggy most of the time due to the pain meds which kept me sleeping for hours at a time. Tim sat by my side and brought me my meals. If I tried to talk, he would just put his finger on my lips and tell me to just rest. On the third day, he said, "I've got to go. He kneeled down, kissed me on my forehead, prayed for me, and left. We didn't talk much. I never got the explanation I wanted about why things turned out the way they did between me and him. There was one thing that I did get. One morning I woke up and the hurt was gone.

The breakup was probably one of the best things that ever happened to me. There is a scripture in Isaiah 55:8–9 (KJV) that says, "For my thoughts are not your thoughts, and your ways are not my ways, this is the Lord's declaration." That simply means, Father knows best.

Chapter 10
A Change of Pace

It was a new year, 1976. I wondered what the New Year would bring. All of my friends had gone back to college after the Christmas break and most of them had chosen schools out of the city. I was missing my oldest sister Kathy who had also gone back to school. We had shared a bedroom since we were babies. When she left for school, I was happy for her as she had received a theater arts scholarship. Although I missed her terribly, I looked forward to having the bedroom all to myself.

We were eleven months apart and were very close. Even though we both had our own circle of friends, we considered ourselves to be best friends and did almost everything together.

I was still recovering from surgery and was not yet quite healed enough to register for the spring semester before the deadline. I stayed at home and was pretty much unproductive during that time. I began to grow bored and restless with each passing day. I didn't know what to do with myself or which direction I wanted to go in, but I knew it was definitely time for a change.

One night as I got into bed, I was feeling a bit discouraged about my circumstances, and I started to cry. I prayed to the Lord to help me. Even though I wasn't sure what I wanted, I knew I needed a change of some kind. As I was finishing my prayer, the phone rang. It was my friend, Annette. She excitedly told me she had a job she thought I would be interested in. Boy, did I perk up! She had no idea how restless and bored I had been feeling.

Annette was going to school at SWTU (Southwest Texas State University) and was working at San Marcos Baptist Academy. She explained the job was for a proctor in a girl's dormitory where she was working. The job only paid thirty-five dollars a month, but room and board were free. She went on to explain that tuition was also paid for students attending the university. Annette said she had already told her supervisor about me and set me up for the interview. I could hardly believe my ears. Wow! The Lord had answered my prayer that fast.

The next morning I told my parents about the phone call, and they were just as excited as I was. They encouraged me to go and felt this was just what I needed. The interview went well, and I was offered the job. Not only was I going to start a new job, but as soon as the summer session rolled around, I could also register for classes at Southwest Texas State. I loved my new job. My responsibilities as a proctor entailed supervising the girl's dormitory in the evening from 4 p.m. to 9 p.m. as well as ground duty, which meant we walked around the campus grounds. I loved ground duty, especially when the weather was good. The campus was so beautiful, I saw being a proctor as a perfect opportunity to witness to the students about the Lord.

One of the rules prohibited fraternizing with the students. I didn't think telling them about Jesus or praying with them was fraternizing, especially since I was told in my interview that all of the staff members were Christians. I got along well with all the students. When the girls got out of class, they came straight to the dormitory. Some of the students would be off doing extracurricular activities. Some would go hang out with other students who were housed in other dorms. In addition, there were always those students who would come and hang out at my desk just to talk and tell me about their day.

Quiet time began at 7 p.m. each evening. This was the time set aside for students to do their homework or study for their exams. No talking or moving around from room to room was permitted during quiet time.

Inevitably, one of the girls would find themselves at my desk in tears about something, seeking my advice. I would give them a listening ear for a few minutes and then remind them they needed to be in their room. Sometimes, I would take a moment to pray with them if I felt the problem they were sharing with me warranted it. When my shift was over I would always stop by that student's room to make sure they were okay and tell them if they still needed to talk, we could talk more about it the next day during my shift.

One day I was told the dean of the academy needed to see me. Although she was somewhat friendly, there were times when she was very stern. I had no idea why she needed to see me. To my surprise, she wanted to let me know she had been getting reports that I was becoming too "chummy" with the students and for me to remember there was to be no fraternizing with the students. I assured her I understood and would do my best to continue to comply with all the guidelines and policies. I loved my job and did not want to get fired.

I tried my best to stick to just doing my job. I have always been outgoing, friendly, and open. The students flocked to me and made it clear they were always happy when I was on duty. I tried to tone down the friendliness and not be so "chummy" with them as well as making sure I was in compliance with the rules. One night during quiet time, one of the students came to my desk very emotionally distraught and fell into my arms crying hysterically. I quickly tried to quiet her down so the others were not disturbed. I chose to let her cry in my arms until she calmed down. After a few minutes, I prayed with her and then insisted she get back to her room as I didn't want her to get into trouble. In the back of my mind, I recall thinking to myself *"Oh dear, I'm probably in trouble now."*

As my shift ended, I felt a strong urgency to check on her right away. I thought to myself, *I'll just stick my head in the door for a quick second but not go inside.* As I opened the door, she had a handful of pills and was about to swallow them. This student did not have a roommate like some of the other girls. Without even thinking about it, I went into her room and pulled her hand down from her mouth. She had pills all over the floor and kept saying she wanted to die. I was going to have to report this and suggest to the room mother coming on duty that this student might need to go to the infirmary.

It appeared as if she had already swallowed some of the pills. I sat with her awhile listening to her woes. I shared with her my own attempt to commit suicide and the miracle of how the Lord allowed me to live. I witnessed to her about the love of God and how He had a purpose for her life, encouraging her to invite Jesus to come into her life. I stayed with her until I felt she was calm enough for me to leave her. I was headed back to my desk to write a report about what happened when someone came and told me the dean wanted to see me immediately. My heart sank, I knew I was in trouble. It was 10 p.m. I wondered what the dean was doing on duty so late and who called her so quickly?

The room mother had been on the floor just a few minutes. When I reached the dean's room, I didn't even give her a chance to tell me what she wanted. I quickly began to tell her what happened. The dean listened intently and expressed her concern for the girl but told me it was my last warning. She made it very clear to me, if there was another infraction I would be terminated immediately. I think she intended to fire me when she summoned me to come to her office, but it would have left her looking as if she did not have any concern for the student who had just tried to commit suicide. She knew my intervention may have saved her life.

When I left the office, I was confused. I knew the Lord had me in the right place at the right time and that the urgency I sensed was from the Holy Spirit. It was God's way of thwarting the plan of the enemy to destroy her.

I was off the next day. I spent most of the day praying about my job. I wanted to check on the student to see how she was doing, but I knew I dared not. Later on that evening, there was a knock on my door. When I opened the door, I was surprised to see that same student standing there. I thought, *Oh no, I'm really going to get fired now*. I quickly asked her what was she doing in the proctor's dorm and whether she knew she could get in a lot of trouble. She told me she didn't care if she got in trouble and said she just had to come and find me.

She went on to explain she wanted to thank me for saving her life. The most important thing that she wanted to tell me was she prayed after I left and invited Jesus to come into her heart. She was gleaming with joy. It was very apparent a change had come over her. I hugged her and rejoiced with her. After she left my room, I shed tears of joy. I was so honored to have been used by the Lord. I was especially happy to hear she had given her life to the Lord.

The next day I felt a little anxious. I kept wondering if word had gotten back to the dean that the student had come to my room. I knew how important it was for me to obey the rules and to respect my boss, but deep down inside I knew if another student came to me in a crisis, wanting prayer, advice, or just a listening ear, I would not be able to turn them away. In a next couple of months, after much prayer about the matter, I chose to resign. I had been there for a year. My sister Kathy had been contemplating moving out of her dormitory, so we both decided the time was perfect for us to move into an apartment together. My baby sister Cynthia would eventually join us. We had a blast living college life together and creating so many fun memories together.

Even though the job didn't work out, I knew God had led me to San Marcos. I wanted change, and change surely came. This change would lead me to a new church where I would learn how to apply the Word of God to my life and go to another plateau in my walk with the Lord. While at SWT, I pledged a sorority (Alpha Kappa Alpha) and was crowned Miss Black Southwest Texas. I would meet and marry my first husband, give birth to my firstborn child, and graduate from college with my bachelor's degree in criminal justice in 1979.

A Change Of Pace

Are you bored, restless and longing for a change in your life? Proverbs 3:5 says if you acknowledge the Lord in all your ways, He will direct your paths. In the book of Psalms, there is a verse in chapter 37 that says as you delight yourself in the Lord, He will give you the desires of your heart. Deep in your heart, you may have something you desire to do or a place you want to go that you have never shared with anyone. I want you to know the Lord knows it's there and desires to give it to you. He is waiting for you to seek Him, tell Him all about it, asking Him for it in faith. He has great things in store for you. His plans for you will not bring you harm but will prosper you and give you a hope and a future. It just may be time for a change of pace.

Chapter 11

His Miracles Never Cease

*I*n April of 1976, just five months after the ovarian surgery, I was back in the hospital again. I found a lump in my breast about the size of a fifty-cent piece. I would have to have surgery again. The first thought I had to deal with was, *the cancer is back.* I remembered the doctors predicted the cancer could return in about three years, and it had been exactly three years. I was still recovering from the last operation, and the thought of going through another operation was very depressing.

The Bible says God has not given me a spirit of fear, but of power, love, and a sound mind. I knew the first thing I needed to do was deal with my fear. Fear is the opposite of faith, and it will paralyze you if you allow it. I took authority over fear and put the spirit of fear in its place, commanding it to shut its mouth in the name of Jesus! I cast down the thoughts that tried to bombard my mind that told me the cancer had returned. I was reminded of a promise in God's Word stating "And whatever you ask in My name, that I will do, that the Father may be glorified in the Son, if you ask anything in My name I will do it." John 14:13–14 (NKJV). I believed God's Word, so I decided I was not going to have another operation. I went to my Heavenly Father and asked for a miracle. I asked the elders at the church to pray for me, and I went on a fast. As the elders were praying for me, the Holy Spirit assured me I had nothing to worry about. Once again, I felt the Lord wrap His loving arms around me and give me His peace.

The day came for me to be admitted into the hospital. It was on a Sunday. Surgery was scheduled for 6 a.m. the next day. I was speaking at a Women's Day program that morning. As I ended my message, I told the congregation that I would be leaving from there to go to the hospital where I was scheduled to have surgery the following morning. I boldly told them I was expecting a miracle and that I believed there would be no surgery. I made this public confession as an act of releasing my faith.

As I was entering the hospital, I was doubled over with sharp pains in my breast. I could not stand up straight for several minutes. My mother jokingly said, "Ava, maybe the Lord just operated on you, and you're not going to have to have the surgery." I responded by telling her I asked for a miracle, and that is what I was expecting.

After getting admitted and settled into my room, both the anesthesiologist and the surgeon came to see me as is the procedure before an operation. The next morning the nurse woke me up at 4 a.m. to get me prepped for surgery. Though the surgeon had come the night before, he was back at my bedside again. He explained he wanted to show me where the incisions were going to be made, so I would know what to expect. The doctor could not find the lump and asked me to find the lump, and I couldn't find it, either. We never had to search for it before. The doctor examined me again and then asked the nurse to wheel me down to the examination room.

After examining me again, he asked another doctor to come in and examine me. That doctor didn't feel anything. I was due to have surgery at 6 a.m. He asked for my file to be sent to the examination room and that I be taken to radiology to have another picture taken of my breast. When I came back from X-ray, he put both films up against the light in order to read them. The mass was clearly seen in one picture, but there was no sign of it in the second picture. I shared with the doctor that I wasn't a bit surprised. I had prayed and asked the Lord to heal me and He did.

They were dumbfounded—completely baffled. There would be no operation. Praise God! I thought for sure I would be released and sent home that same day, but my doctor ordered more tests. I would have to stay another three days until the results were back. Each test came back negative. I had been healed before, but this healing was on a different level. It was a miracle!

Jesus provided healing for us when He was whipped, receiving thirty-nine stripes across his back. The Word of God tells us we were healed by His stripes. Have you or a loved one been diagnosed with a serious illness? Ask Jesus that the healing He has already provided for you to be manifested in your body. Nothing is too hard for God! He is able to do more than we can ask or think. Trust Him and *expect a miracle.*

Chapter 12

He Will Perfect That Which Concerns You

*A*fter moving out of the academy and into an apartment with my sister, I became a full-time student at Southwest Texas State. This was a big accomplishment for me since I had struggled through school most of my life. All through high school, I basically made C's and in math, D's and sometimes an F. It did not matter how hard I studied or how often I was tutored, I just couldn't pass math and never seemed to be able to get an A in anything.

I took the college entrance exams, but my score was always too low for most of the universities. I was able to attend the junior college under the remedial program. This meant I had to take remedial classes and pass them. I did not get any credit for them, but it would cancel my low SAT score and allow me to transfer to a four-year college.

I was excited about being a full-time student but nervous about being able to make the required grades.

I was attending Hill Country Faith Ministries where I learned so much about the Word of God and how to apply it to my life. There, I met two precious and powerful women of God, Mildred and Ruth. These two ladies took me under their wing and taught me how to pray, who I was in Christ, and most of all how to operate effectively in spiritual warfare. The greatest knowledge I learned while under their tutelage was that I was victorious in Christ and that God would always cause me to triumph no matter what I was facing.

One particular semester, I was taking an American History class. It was rumored that the professor teaching the class was one of the hardest professors on the campus and that "A" students had trouble passing his class. After hearing this, I wanted to drop the class because if the "A" students had difficulty passing his class, surely as an average student, I would not be able to pass his class. The morning I planned to go and drop the class, a scripture kept coming to the forefront of my mind. It was Philippians 4:13 (KJV) that says, "I can do all things through Christ who strengthens me." I said to myself, *Okay, Ava, if you believe the Word of God, this means you can pass the class, and Christ will give you the strength to do it.*

I determined in my heart and mind that I was going to stand on this scripture and pass this class with flying colors. I had also read in the scriptures that faith without works was dead. I decided to write the scripture on an index card and tape it to my mirror. I prayed and asked the Lord to help me and told Him because I believed His Word, I was not going to drop the class. Every morning when I woke up, I would quote the scripture out loud. I would not just quote the scripture but I also began thanking the Lord for my passing grade as well. If you pray about something, pray in faith and then thank the Lord for it as if you already have the answer to your prayer.

I didn't just pray and quote scripture, I also studied more diligently than I ever had before. This time, it was with a different attitude and expectancy. I asked the Lord to help me retain all that I studied. Another verse that helped me during this time was 1 Corinthians 2:16, which says "but we have the mind of Christ." Well, if I have the mind of Christ, surely I could pass a history class. I started applying this scripture to my study time as well.

About two weeks before finals, I caught a bad case of the flu. I tried my best to study but spent most of the time in the bed. I wasn't shaken, though; I was more determined than ever that I was going to pass this class.

Finally, it was time to take my final exams. I was concerned about my grades but because my Heavenly Father promised me in Psalm 138:8 (AKJV), "The Lord will perfect that which concerns me," I made an A on the final and an overall B in the class. What a mighty God we serve! Not only did I pass my history class with a B but I made A's and B's in all my other classes. For the first time, I made the dean's list and stayed on the dean's list until I graduated in 1979 with a BS degree in criminal justice. To God be the glory!

As I close out this chapter, I am reminded of a song titled, "What a Friend we have in Jesus." I love the lyric that says, "What a privilege to carry, everything to God in prayer." As I continue to go from glory to glory, I have learned to pray about everything and to cast my cares on Him because he cares for me.

Know that God cares for you and He invites you to come to Him with your concerns. Wait in faith, and watch Him perfect all of your trepidations.

Chapter 13

He Supplies All of My Needs

*T*he Lord has done so many great things in my life. Though there have been times when I have not been steadfast and my faith has wavered, Yeshua (the name Jesus in Hebrew) has remained faithful to His promises. He has shown Himself to be reliable, trustworthy, constant, unfailing, unwavering, and steadfast. One of the names of God, is Jehovah Jireh, or Yahweh Yireh, which means "the Lord will provide." He has indeed always provided for me.

I am reminded of a time when I had no money and did not know how I was going to pay my bills. I was in college living in an apartment with my sister and one of my sorority sisters. We always divided the bills three ways. The day finally came for both my roommates to graduate, which meant they would be moving out. After the excitement of graduation celebrations had worn off, it was time for the bills to be paid and I had to pay them all by myself. There was hardly any food in the refrigerator. The money I received for school usually would cover rent, bills, books, and tuition; but it was not scheduled to be disbursed until September, and it was only June. Although I was working

He Supplies All Of My Needs

at the time, it was only a part-time job. I could have called my father, but I was on my own and didn't want to do that.

After tossing and turning all night trying to figure out what I was going to do, I got up that morning and tearfully got on my knees to pray. I asked the Lord to forgive me for being so fretful and anxious. I had spent the night worrying about it instead of coming to Him with it. I cried my heart out to Him about my concerns and then asked Him to move the mountain I was facing. As I was praying about it, I resolved in my heart and mind I was going to trust Him to work it out. Once I made that decision, I felt a peace come over me. I got up from my knees, dried my tears, got dressed, and went to class. I was confident that the Lord was going to meet my needs. I reminded myself that I served a big God and no problem was too big for him. I had no idea how it was going to work out; I just knew the Lord was going to open a door of provision.

When I returned from class, as I was opening the door to my apartment, the phone was ringing. It was the secretary from my church, Hill Country Faith Ministries. She said there was an envelope with my name on it there and asked when I could come and pick it up. She couldn't answer any of my questions about the envelope or who it was from. She told me she was instructed to call me and ask me to come pick it up.

When I opened the envelope I started crying and shouting for joy all at the same time. The envelope was full of money. I had no idea who gave it to me. The Bible says the righteous never have to beg for bread. There was enough money in the envelope to pay all the bills for the next two months. I had not told one person, not even my parents, about my financial situation. I praised the Lord all the way home.

The next day my father called to tell me he and my mother were coming to visit. When they got there my father told me to get in the car. They took me to the store and brought me enough groceries to last me for the rest of the summer and gave me some money. My cup was running over. Philippians 4:19 (KJV) states, "But my God shall supply all your need according to his riches in glory by Christ Jesus."

On many other occasions, the Lord would not only come to my rescue again and meet a financial need, often He did so supernaturally. In my senior year in college, April 1979, I married my first husband. He was good looking, outgoing and a football player. Everyone knew him, and he knew everyone. I knew I was going to marry him on our first date. We married after dating for two years. We had three wonderful children, Micah Joel, Maresah Jane, and Matthew Jacob. After eight years of marriage, my dream of "living happily ever after" came to an end.

I had a big beautiful wedding with over 300 guest in attendance. Two weeks later the honeymoon was over when I was suddenly jerked out of the shower, slapped around, and called every name but my own. I was stunned. I thought someone had broken into the house and was surprised to find out it was my husband who had just thrown me up against the wall. He told me that I hung his shirts up in the wrong place in the closet. He threw the entire rack of clothes at me.

Later, when things calmed down, he confessed his love for me and promised me it would never happen again. I wanted to believe his promise, so I convinced myself it wouldn't happen again. I told myself to try harder not to do anything to make him angry. Little did I know, it would be the beginning of an eight-year roller coaster ride of separating and getting back together again. I loved my husband very much and wanted to provide a stable home for my children, so I held on to all the "I love you's" as well as the "I'm sorry; I won't do it again" and "if you wouldn't do this, then I wouldn't do that." I was always doing everything I could to try to please him. I was afraid of him and never knew when something I did would cause him to explode.

We separated at least five times in the eight years we were married. Then one morning after another outburst of physical and verbal abuse, my two-year-old daughter asked me, "Mommy, why do you let Daddy do that to you?" I looked at her through tears while she said it again, but this time everything around me froze and I heard "you let" three times over and over. It was the "YOU LET" that got my attention. Something snapped inside of me, and I realized I was enduring something that I could choose to walk away from. I was at my wits end, and it was then that I decided I would not allow this abuse to continue. Once I made that decision, I had perfect peace. I picked up the phone and called my friend Verna to come and get me. I didn't know where I was going to go; I only knew I had to leave. Although Verna promised to come right away but not without telling me if I went back to him again, we could no longer be friends.

She invited me and the children to stay with her until I was able to figure things out. Verna was my prayer partner and my friend. I know God placed her in my life to help me get through a very tough season. She walked through it with me, holding my arms up when I didn't think I could go on. Verna's prayers, love, and support helped me each day to put one foot in front of the other and keep moving. I love you, Verna, and will forever be grateful to you for how you came to my rescue that day and how you always stood with me through thick and thin. During my stay with her, the Lord showed Himself to be a supernatural God.

I chose to leave everything behind. I only packed a diaper bag and left with the clothes on our backs. When I walked out of the door that day, my mind was made up. I knew this time I would not be coming back. I didn't know how I would provide for my children but I knew the Lord would take care of us. I called some friends that lived in Portland, Texas, near Corpus Christi and told them what was happening, and they invited me to come stay with them for a couple of months.

The following day, I asked Verna to take me to the bank because I would be leaving town and wanted to withdraw some money. I could have withdrawn everything in the bank because I still had three children to care for, but I only withdrew $100.00. I was afraid to even take that much. I decided the first thing I wanted to do was to tithe from that money as well as give an offering. I got a money order in the amount of $18.00 and mailed it to my church. I had $82.00 left.

I asked Verna to take me to a place where I needed to get something out of layaway. On the way there, we stopped at a friend's store just to say hello and to ask for prayer. When we walked in he said, "I've been expecting you this morning." He instructed me to look on his desk where there was an envelope with my name on it. He went on to explain he had prayed over the envelope and that the Lord was going to do something supernatural in my life that day in reference to my money. He also said that I was to take what he had given me and treat myself to something special and asked me not to use it on a necessity. I thanked him and let him know how grateful I was.

When we left my friend's store, we stopped at another store where I did just what he asked and bought something

He Supplies All Of My Needs

for myself. We proceeded on to the store where I had the layaway. Remember after mailing off my tithe and offering, I had exactly $82.00. I gave Verna two one dollar bills to help with gas. The layaway was $16.94. I reached in my wallet and pulled out a twenty-dollar bill. I dropped the change in my purse, not putting it directly in my wallet.

The next stop we made was to a thrift store to buy the kids and me a few clothing items. That bill cost another $17.00. I went into my wallet and pulled out another twenty-dollar bill but as I reached for it I noticed I had four twenty-dollar bills. I had already used two of the twenty-dollar bills and should not have had $80.00. I shrugged my shoulders and thought maybe I was mistaken. I paid the bill and dropped the change down into my purse.

When I got back to the car, I told my friend unless I had miscounted, I seemed to have more money in my wallet than I should. I counted the money in my wallet. I had four twenty-dollar bills. I should have had only two twenty-dollar bills left. I let my friend count it to make sure I was not hallucinating. We left there and went to eat and to the grocery store, HEB. Both times I pulled a twenty-dollar bill out of my wallet, not wanting to search for the change I had been dropping down in my purse with each transaction. When we got back to Verna's house, I still had four twenty-dollar bills. I also had about thirty dollars from each time I had been given change. This was a miracle. I was in awe of God.

The next day I went to see my lawyer about filing for a divorce. I was concerned I would not be able to afford her fee. After consulting with her about what I had gone through she said, "Well, I don't want you to worry about my retainer. I'm going to waive it. I will only need you to pay $80.00 for the filing fees." I couldn't believe my ears.

Did she just say all she needed was $80.00? Verna and I looked at each other and smiled. I had that exact amount—$80.00. God had supernaturally provided it.

A wonderful family, Ron and Tonia Woolever from Portland, Texas, took care of my children and me while I made the transition to single parenthood. I have so many testimonies about what happened while living there. The Lord was so good to me and made sure we did not lack anything. After staying with the Woolever's for a few months, I was able to move into my own apartment. My first night there I wasn't sure how I was going to feed my children. I had very little money and barely any food in the cabinets. Someone knocked on our door, when I answered it, and there stood a group of people who came in with enough groceries to last us for at least a month.

After about seven months in Portland and my divorce was final, I decided to move back to San Antonio. I lived with my parents for a short while until I was able to find a job and get a place to live of my own. I also found a new church home that I absolutely loved—New Life Christian Center. Dr. LaSalle Vaughn was the pastor, and his wife, Portia Brooks Vaughn, was the co-pastor. It was at this church, I would go to the next level in my spiritual growth. One day my pastor asked the congregation to bring two canned goods to the next service. As I was taking the two cans out of my pantry, I heard the Holy Spirit tell me to empty my cabinets and take all the canned goods I had to church. I didn't hesitate as I recognized the voice of the Lord and knew to be obedient.

Later that month, after receiving a good evaluation from my supervisor, without warning I lost my job. The explanation I was given was they had decided to do something different with the department. I was able to receive

He Supplies All Of My Needs

unemployment for a period of time, but it ran out before I found another job. One Saturday after a meeting at my church, Pastor Vaughn asked me how I was doing. I responded by telling him I was doing fine, but he wanted to know how I was "really doing" and encouraged me to tell him how things were going in my life. At that point, I decided to be honest with him and told him the unemployment had just run out, I wasn't receiving any child support, and I had not found a job yet. He prayed with me and told me to keep trusting God and to stay encouraged. The following day, he asked the congregation to bring back to the evening service a bag of groceries. I remember my pastor telling the congregation to put things in the bag that they would want to eat and to be sure and put some meat in it.

I didn't have much money, but I bought a small bag of groceries as well. When I walked into the foyer that Sunday night, there was hardly any room to walk. There were grocery bags everywhere. I could barely find an empty space to put my bag down. After church, one of the members asked me whether she could borrow my car so she could deliver the groceries and whether I would mind waiting there at the church until she returned. There were so many groceries that they needed two cars. When she returned, she told me they needed to take another load, but this time she asked could I drive the car because the groceries were actually for me. Oh my goodness! I had no idea they were for me! I couldn't believe it.

As usual, whenever, I experience the hand of God moving in my life, I began to cry tears of joy, thanking and praising God all at the same time. When I got in the car, the trunk was full, the back seat was full, the floor of the car was full, and this was the second load. My children had to sit in the front seat. The lady who had asked to borrow my car was my landlord, so she had a key to my house. She had taken the first load from both cars into the house and put them up. The freezer in the garage was filled with meat, my refrigerator was full of food, milk, and juice; and my cabinets were filled to capacity. I had so many groceries left over that I had to give some of them away because I didn't have anywhere to put them. I believe if I had not been obedient to the Holy Spirit who instructed me to empty my cabinets that day we were asked to bring two canned goods back to church, I would not have been the recipient of such an abundant blessing.

The New Living Translation of Luke 6:38 says, "Give and you will receive. Your gift will return to you in full-pressed down, shaken together to make room for more, running over and poured into your lap. The amount you give will determine the amount you get back." This surely was a running-over blessing, and it was definitely poured into my lap. To God be the glory for the great things He has done.

Pastor LaSalle R. Vaughn and Co-Pastor Portia Brooks-Vaughn were my pastors at that time. I am so grateful for how Pastor Vaughn took the time that day to ask me how I was "really doing." I'm so thankful that the Lord brought such awesome pastors into my life. I reached a new level of spiritual maturity while under their tutelage. I will always love them and will be forever grateful for how they watched over my soul. They were always there for me, praying with me and encouraging me to keep standing. They taught me how to reach my full potential in God.

Do you have a financial need in your life? I encourage you to find something to give away in faith, believing that all your needs are met in Christ Jesus. I promise, you will not go lacking and that Jehovah Jireh will provide.

Chapter 14

We Are More than Conquerors

It is God's desire that we love Him with all our hearts and allow Him to love us. Jesus came that we might have life and have it more abundantly. God has taken me from one level of glory to another level of glory, allowing each problem, hurt, disappointment, and trial to transform me into the image of His son, Jesus Christ. I've come through each situation in victory and as a result, I am much stronger in my faith. Everything I have been through, though Satan meant it for evil and tried to destroy me, God turned it around and allowed it to work for my good.

You too, can come through your trials victoriously. There are some Christians who have the assurance of going to heaven but do not understand who they are in Christ and that they are equipped with everything they need to live a victorious life in spite of the trials they may face. Romans 8:38–39 *(NKJV)* reminds us

> Who shall separate us from the love of Christ? Shall tribulation, or distress, or persecution, or famine, or nakedness or peril

or sword?" As it is written, "For your sake we are killed all day long; we are accounted as sheep for the slaughter." Yet in all these things we are more than conquerors through Him who loved us. For I am persuaded that neither death nor life, nor angels nor principalities nor powers, nor things present nor things to come, nor height nor depth, nor any other created thing, shall be able to separate us from the love of God which is in Christ Jesus our Lord.

If you have a problem, speak to your mountain in the name of Jesus, and command it to move as Jesus instructed in Matthew 17:20. Then release your faith. Stand on God's Word. Don't just hope that one day things will work out but *know* that God (Jehovah Jireh) will provide. He will save (Jehovah Rapha), He will heal, He will deliver, He will love, He will forgive, and most of all, the Most High God is sovereign and is therefore in control. Yahweh is the one true God. The name Yeshua (Jesus) is above every name. He is Wonderful Counselor, the Bright and Morning Star, the Prince of Peace, our Redeemer. If you ever feel like you don't know how to pray and are in a crisis, just say His name, for at the very mention of His name, the demons tremble.

If you don't know Jesus Christ as your personal Lord and Savior, let me invite you to accept Him right now. He loves you. He gave His life for you. The most exciting news is after dying on the cross, He conquered death, rose from the dead, and lives so that you might also live. He will accept you just as you are. Invite Him to come into your heart by praying this prayer:

> Dear God, I confess that I am a sinner and I repent and ask for your forgiveness. I believe Jesus Christ is Your Son. I believe that He died for my sins and that you raised Him from the dead. I want to trust Jesus as my Savior and follow you as Lord from this day forward. Take control of my life. Your will be done in my life.

If you prayed this prayer, you are now a child of God and part of the Body of Christ. Find a friend who is a Christian and ask them to help you find a good church to attend where you can have someone to pray with you and disciple you as you begin your new life in Christ.

To those of you who already know Jesus, let me encourage you to keep standing, keep believing, and keep your eyes on Jesus. Don't allow circumstances to torment you and get you off course. Continue to endure and persevere. If you fall down, get up and keep running the race the Lord has set before you. If you've backed away from the Lord, return to Him, your first love. He is waiting to receive you with open arms. Draw near to Him, and He will draw near to you. His love is eternal, and there is nothing you can do to stop the Lord from loving you.

As a believer, a child of God, you have authority over the powers of darkness in the name of Jesus. There is power in the name of Jesus. Stand on God's Word according to the instructions found in chapter 6 of the book of Ephesians. Release your faith, and speak the Word to your problem until you see a change. When God's Word is sent out, He promises to watch over His Word so that it will perform what it was sent out to do. But you have to send the Word out. In order to do that, you have to read your Bible, so you know what promises are available to you.

When I am facing a financial situation, I find scriptures that have to do with God's promise of provision. If I am sick, I look for scriptures that have to do with the promise of healing. I confess the Word of God over my circumstances and release my faith. I exercise my faith by thanking the Lord until I see the full manifestation of His Word come to pass in my life.

Someone asked me how I became such a strong Christian. I told them it was because I finally discovered who I was in Christ. I decided to walk in the truth that I am more than a conqueror through Christ Jesus. That same Spirit that raised Christ from the dead dwells within me. Since Jesus conquered death, I can conquer any challenge I face. I go from glory to glory and am able to conquer my problems. I am sufficient in Christ. I am well able to endure, battle, and conquer with God as my ally; and my faith in Him serves as my shield. I am convinced God is faithful and is on my side. He is in me, He is for me, and He is with me.

One day while in prayer, I was telling the Lord I wanted more of Him. While praying, I had a vision of a body of water that appeared to be the ocean. Then I heard the Lord say to me, "If you want more of me, come to me." Jesus was standing in the middle of the ocean. I looked again and said to myself, "I never learned to swim, and for many years I have been afraid of the water. He knows I'm afraid of water." Again the Lord said to me if you want more of me, come to me. I focused my eyes on Jesus and began to slowly get into the water. I knew I had to keep my eyes on Him or else the fear I had of the water would cause me to turn back. I kept moving through the water and just as the level of the water was below my nose, Jesus took my hand and pulled me out of the water.

The scene changed. I was in the middle of an earthquake. I could see the streets opening up, buildings crumbling all around me, and I could hear people screaming. I looked up and the Lord was standing in the middle of all of the chaos. He beckoned for me to come to him, saying if I wanted more of Him to come to where he was. Though I was afraid, I moved toward him. I knew if I locked my eyes on Him, I would be okay as long as I did not turn my head to look at all that was happening around me. Just as the street began to open up under me, Jesus reached out and grabbed my hand, preventing me from falling.

Suddenly, the scenery changed, and I was looking at a fire that had gotten out of control. The flames were blazing hot and very high. Then I saw Jesus standing in the middle of one of the flames. He said if you want more of me, then come. His arms were outstretched for me to join him in the flame. I didn't move right away, but my heart filled with such a strong desire to serve the Lord no matter what, and I heard him say once again, if you want more of me, come. As I slowly moved into the fire, I saw that I was not being consumed by the fire. I kept my focus on His eyes. Then all the fear left me, and I had perfect peace.

After that, I saw that it was a beautiful day. There were beautiful flowers and trees everywhere. I could hear the birds singing. I was in the middle of the ocean, and Jesus was standing on the shore. As I got closer to the shore, He gave me His hand to help me out of the water and said, "Now as I have overcome the world, so shall you." I later found a scripture in the book of Isaiah 43:2 (NIV) that states:

> When you pass through the waters, I will be with you; and when you pass through the rivers, they will not sweep over you. When you walk through the fire, you will not be burned; the flames will not set you ablaze.

I want to leave you with one more scripture that has encouraged me many times through thick and thin. My prayer is that it will be an encouragement to you, too, as you go from glory to glory throughout your life. Second Corinthians 4:8, 16 (NKJV) says:

> We are hard pressed on every side, yet not crushed, we are perplexed, but not in despair, persecuted but not forsaken, struck down, but not destroyed. . . . Do not lose heart. Never throw away your confidence in God.

When my father died in 1995, I could not imagine how I would be able to get through the loss of my father and while feeling as if my heart was broken into a million pieces, the Lord gently spoke to me saying, "My grace is sufficient for you." His grace is sufficient for you also. Go forth and be victorious.

After my divorce, my confidence was shaken, causing me to fear the Lord would not be able to use me in ministry. I often wondered if I would find love again. At times, I would hear over and over again in my mind the awful names I was called and the words my ex spoke over me. "No one is ever going to want you," he would say.

To God be the glory! After I found Jesus to be the lover of my soul first, seven years after my divorce, I met a man who is the love of my life; Earl Clifton Fulmer. I call him my "chocolate honey." When he joined New Life Christian Center, he told me one day during one of the services, "When my eyes fell on you as I watched you worship the Lord, I knew right away you were a woman of God." Little did he know, after dating different men off and on for seven years, I had made up in my mind I was not dating anymore until the Lord sent me the man I was to marry.

I told the Lord, "The only way I will know that You have sent a man into my life, is if he would say to me, "I know you are a woman of God." My husband told me he was going to marry me even before we had our first date. Of course I protested thinking, *this guy is crazy*, and then he insisted that I go out with him just one time. I thought he was awfully arrogant. Well, he was right. I fell head over heels in love with him.

He had three children, Tammy, Chasity, and Shawn. I also had three children. We blended our families together and are now proud grandparents of fifteen grandchildren. This year we are celebrating our 25th wedding anniversary. I am as much in love with him today as I was the day I married him. In 2009, my husband and I answered the call to go into full time ministry. We are now pastors of The Clarion Call Christian Center.

About the Author

Ava Hornsby Fulmer graduated from Southwest Texas State in 1979 with a degree in criminal justice and a minor in psychology. She was called into the ministry and went on to attend and graduate from New Living Word Seminary in 1996. She was licensed and ordained in 2009. She also attended and graduated from the Five Fold School of Ministry Seminary.

She is a wife, mother, and grandmother. Pastor Ava serves at the Clarion Christian Center alongside her husband Senior Pastor Earl Fulmer, preaching and teaching the Gospel.

She worked for many years as a program director, recruiter, trainer, and developer. She also actively participated in Operation Outcry with the Texas Justice Foundation, sharing her painful experience about her abortion and how abortion hurts. She has been on numerous talk shows sharing her testimony of God's grace, healing, and forgiveness.

Ava is the founder of Glory to Glory Workshops, which are geared to help women recover from life's hurting trials. Along with her sister, Cynthia Hornsby, she hosts a citywide annual Christian Women's Fellowship called *A Love Fest with Jesus*.

Ava has a heart for women and is passionate about teaching them who they are in Christ. She has a desire to equip them to become all they can be in God. When facing life's challenges, she draws strength from the Word of God and meditates especially on Micah 7:7–8 that states:

> Therefore I will look unto the Lord: I will wait for the God of my Salvation: My God will hear me. Rejoice not against me, O mine enemy, when I fall I shall arise; when I sit in darkness, the Lord shall be a light unto me. (KJV)

Printed in the USA
CPSIA information can be obtained
at www.ICGtesting.com
LVHW090342230524
780924LV00001B/168